Food Systems in Africa

Food Systems in Africa

Rethinking the Role of Markets

**Gaëlle Balineau, Arthur Bauer,
Martin Kessler, and Nicole Madariaga**

A copublication of the Agence française de développement and the World Bank

Interior design and layout: Coquelicot
Cover design: Bill Pragluski, Critical Stages LLC

ISBN (paper): 978-1-4648-1588-1
ISBN (electronic): 978-1-4648-1589-8
DOI: 10.1596/978-1-4648-1588-1

Cover photo: Fish Market, Essaouira, Morocco. License CC0.
https://www.piqsels.com/en/public-domain-photo-orpz.

The Library of Congress control number has been requested.

Africa Development Forum Series

The **Africa Development Forum Series** was created in 2009 to focus on issues of significant relevance to Sub-Saharan Africa's social and economic development. Its aim is both to record the state of the art on a specific topic and to contribute to ongoing local, regional, and global policy debates. It is designed specifically to provide practitioners, scholars, and students with the most up-to-date research results while highlighting the promise, challenges, and opportunities that exist on the continent.

The series is sponsored by Agence française de développement and the World Bank. The manuscripts chosen for publication represent the highest quality in each institution and have been selected for their relevance to the development agenda. Working together with a shared sense of mission and interdisciplinary purpose, the two institutions are committed to a common search for new insights and new ways of analyzing the development realities of the Sub-Saharan Africa region.

Advisory Committee Members

Agence française de développement
Thomas Mélonio, Executive Director, Research and Knowledge Directorate
Hélène Djoufelkit, Director, Economic Assessment and Public Policy Department
Marie-Pierre Nicollet, Director, Knowledge Department on Sustainable Development
Sophie Chauvin, Head, Edition and Publication Division

World Bank
Albert G. Zeufack, Chief Economist, Africa Region
Markus P. Goldstein, Lead Economist, Africa Region
Zainab Usman, Public Sector Specialist, Africa Region

Sub-Saharan Africa

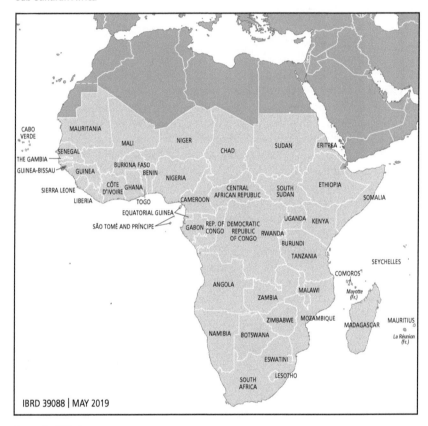

IBRD 39088 | MAY 2019

Source: World Bank.

Titles in the Africa Development Forum Series

2020

The Future of Work in Africa: Harnessing the Potential of Digital Technologies for All (2020), Jieun Choi, Mark Dutz, Zainab Usman (eds.)

Food Systems in Africa: Rethinking the Role of Markets (2020), *Les systèmes agro-alimentaires en Afrique : repenser le rôle des marchés* (2020), Gaëlle Balineau, Arthur Bauer, Martin Kessler, Nicole Madariaga

2019

Electricity Access in Sub-Saharan Africa: Uptake, Reliability, and Complementary Factors for Economic Impact (2019), *Accès à l'électricité en Afrique subsaharienne : adoption, fiabilité et facteurs complémentaires d'impact économique* (2020), Moussa P. Blimpo, Malcolm Cosgrove-Davies

The Skills Balancing Act in Sub-Saharan Africa: Investing in Skills for Productivity, Inclusivity, and Adaptability (2019), *Le développement des competencies en Afrique subsaharienne, un exercice d'équilibre : investir dans les compétences pour la productivité, l'inclusion et l'adaptabilité* (2020), Omar Arias, David K. Evans, Indhira Santos

All Hands on Deck: Reducing Stunting through Multisectoral Efforts in Sub-Saharan Africa (2019), Emmanuel Skoufias, Katja Vinha, Ryoko Sato

2018

Realizing the Full Potential of Social Safety Nets in Africa (2018), Kathleen Beegle, Aline Coudouel, Emma Monsalve (eds.)

Facing Forward: Schooling for Learning in Africa (2018), *Perspectives : l'école au service de l'apprentissage en Afrique* (2019), Sajitha Bashir, Marlaine Lockheed, Elizabeth Ninan, Jee-Peng Tan

2017

Reaping Richer Returns: Public Spending Priorities for African Agriculture Productivity Growth (2017), *Obtenir de meilleurs résultats : priorités en matière de dépenses publiques pour les gains de productivité de l'agriculture africaine* (2020), Aparajita Goyal, John Nash

Mining in Africa: Are Local Communities Better Off? (2017), *L'exploitation minière en Afrique : les communautés locales en tirent-elles parti?* (2020), Punam Chuhan-Pole, Andrew L. Dabalen, Bryan Christopher Land

2016

Confronting Drought in Africa's Drylands: Opportunities for Enhancing Resilience (2016), Raffaello Cervigni and Michael Morris (eds.)

2015

Safety Nets in Africa: Effective Mechanisms to Reach the Poor and Most Vulnerable (2015), *Les filets sociaux en Afrique : méthodes efficaces pour cibler les populations pauvres et vulnérables en Afrique subsaharienne* (2015), Carlo del Ninno, Bradford Mills (eds.)

Land Delivery Systems in West African Cities: The Example of Bamako, Mali (2015), *Le système d'approvisionnement en terres dans les villes d'Afrique de l'Ouest : L'exemple de Bamako* (2015), Alain Durand-Lasserve, Maÿlis Durand-Lasserve, Harris Selod

Enhancing the Climate Resilience of Africa's Infrastructure: The Power and Water Sectors (2015), Raffaello Cervigni, Rikard Liden, James E. Neumann, Kenneth M. Strzepek (eds.)

Africa's Demographic Transition: Dividend or Disaster? (2015), *La transition démographique de l'Afrique : dividende ou catastrophe ?* (2016), David Canning, Sangeeta Raja, Abdo Yazbech

The Challenge of Fragility and Security in West Africa (2015), Alexandre Marc, Neelam Verjee, Stephen Mogaka

Highways to Success or Byways to Waste: Estimating the Economic Benefits of Roads in Africa (2015), Ali A. Rubaba, Federico Barra, Claudia Berg, Richard Damania, John Nash, Jason Russ

2014

Youth Employment in Sub-Saharan Africa (2014), *L'emploi des jeunes en Afrique subsaharienne* (2014), Deon Filmer, Louise Fox

Tourism in Africa: Harnessing Tourism for Growth and Improved Livelihoods (2014), Iain Christie, Eneida Fernandes, Hannah Messerli, Louise Twining-Ward

2013

The Political Economy of Decentralization in Sub-Saharan Africa: A New Implementation Model (2013), Bernard Dafflon, Thierry Madiès (eds.)

Empowering Women: Legal Rights and Economic Opportunities in Africa (2013), Mary Hallward-Driemeier, Tazeen Hasan

Les marchés urbains du travail en Afrique subsaharienne (2013), Urban Labor Markets in Sub-Saharan Africa (2013), Philippe De Vreyer, François Roubaud (eds.)

Securing Africa's Land for Shared Prosperity: A Program to Scale Up Reforms and Investments (2013), Frank F. K. Byamugisha

2012

Light Manufacturing in Africa: Targeted Policies to Enhance Private Investment and Create Jobs (2012), *L'Industrie légère en Afrique : politiques ciblées pour susciter l'investissement privé et créer des emplois* (2012), Hinh T. Dinh, Vincent Palmade, Vandana Chandra, Frances Cossar

Informal Sector in Francophone Africa: Firm Size, Productivity, and Institutions (2012), *Les entreprises informelles de l'Afrique de l'ouest francophone : taille, productivité et institutions* (2012), Nancy Benjamin, Ahmadou Aly Mbaye

Financing Africa's Cities: The Imperative of Local Investment (2012), *Financer les villes d'Afrique : l'enjeu de l'investissement local* (2012), Thierry Paulais

Structural Transformation and Rural Change Revisited: Challenges for Late Developing Countries in a Globalizing World (2012), *Transformations rurales et développement : les défis du changement structurel dans un monde globalisé* (2013), Bruno Losch, Sandrine Fréguin-Gresh, Eric Thomas White

2011

Contemporary Migration to South Africa: A Regional Development Issue (2011), Aurelia Segatti, Loren Landau (eds.)

L'Économie politique de la décentralisation dans quatre pays d'Afrique subsaharienne : Burkina Faso, Sénégal, Ghana et Kenya (2011), Bernard Dafflon, Thierry Madiès (eds.)

2010

Africa's Infrastructure: A Time for Transformation (2010), *Infrastructures africaines, une transformation impérative* (2010), Vivien Foster, Cecilia Briceño-Garmendia (eds.)

Gender Disparities in Africa's Labor Market (2010), Jorge Saba Arbache, Alexandre Kolev, Ewa Filipiak (eds.)

Challenges for African Agriculture (2010), Jean-Claude Deveze (eds.)

All books in the Africa Development Forum series that were copublished
by Agence française de développement and the World Bank are available free at
https://openknowledge.worldbank.org/handle/10986/2150
and https://www.afd.fr/fr/collection/lafrique-en-developpement

Contents

Graphs

Maps

Table

Foreword

This volume could be entitled "Long Live the Markets." However, that phrase usually evokes financial markets, whereas this report actually covers physical food markets—the places where the trade and transaction essential for economies and societies in Africa and elsewhere are conducted.

It is revealing that physical rather than financial markets must be specified as this volume's subject, chiefly because the economic and institutional literature on developing countries pays much more attention to financial markets. Thus this volume, jointly published by the World Bank and Agence française de développement, the French development agency, fills an important research gap by examining food supply and distribution infrastructure. In their focus on the upstream and downstream environments of food markets, the authors shed light on a blind spot in the literature—and one that cannot be justified because, as they note, "hunger is gaining ground." Food remains Africans' largest household expense, consuming 44 percent of budgets on average.

The authors' "farm to table" perspective underpins a systemic analysis of food markets that runs through a continuum of actors, from producers to consumers. The authors critique the practice of financing isolated projects that excessively concentrate on production and that neglect logistics, distribution, consumers, and market governance more broadly. National governments and their technical and financial partners are included in this critique, which logically advocates for a more systems-oriented approach to programs that would genuinely strengthen the capacity of African societies to achieve the United Nations' food-related Sustainable Development Goals.

Responses to the COVID-19 pandemic have affected food systems, disrupting national and international supply chains with curfews, travel reductions, and other constraints for overland, air, and marine freight operations. Wholesale and retail food distributors have had to shut down or partially close markets, reducing access for all city dwellers, especially the most vulnerable populations who depend on markets and street vendors. Producers and growers, too, have lost customers and sales, as have traders and small truckers. These often-informal workers have then lost their means of subsistence. The effects of the COVID-19 pandemic on the African continent worry many observers, even though each country's situation differs in the intensity of the crisis, measures taken by its national and local governments, and the effectiveness of its domestic and international food supply and distribution channels.

Enormous food security challenges loom in the wake of the COVID-19 pandemic. According to the World Food Programme's Spring 2020 estimates, the pandemic's knock-on effects could increase the number of East Africans suffering from food insecurity from 20 million in 2020 to 43 million by 2025. This volume will likely be published during the near-term COVID-19 emergency. In the medium term, food system weaknesses uncovered by the pandemic will call for solutions that bolster food system sustainability and resilience. This volume's systems-oriented, structural analysis provides substantive solutions to such issues.

The systemically important role of food markets has been recognized for a very long time. Although some issues confronting contemporary African food systems differ from those of 10 or 20 years ago, others remain constant. Exceedingly high transaction costs between African producers and consumers contribute to a too-high cost of living, by about 30 percent, forcing large swathes of Africans to remain in relative or extreme poverty.

This volume examines food systems in three West African cities—Abidjan (Côte d'Ivoire), Rabat-Salé-Témara (Morocco), and Niamey (Niger)—and confirms the negative country-specific effects of what I might call the "non-markets" of inefficient urban food supply chains. Espousing a dynamic vision of food markets, the authors discuss major trends such as the rapid uptake of information and communications technologies by the food value chain, the effects of such technologies, the rapid development of supermarkets, and the risks associated with climate change and poor governance—trends that call for thinking about tomorrow's food systems today.

Thomas Mélonio
Executive Director, Innovation, Research and Knowledge Directorate
Agence française de développement

Acknowledgments

Gaëlle Balineau, Arthur Bauer, Martin Kessler, and Nicole Madariaga prepared this volume, with contributions from Mohammed Aderghal, Antoine Boyet, Eduardo Brisson, Marie-Françoise Calmette, Jean-René Cuzon, Lou D'Angelo, Alix Françoise, Tarik Harroud, Frédéric Lançon, Sylvaine Lemeilleur, Paule Moustier, Bruno Romagny, and Max Rousseau. The volume was based on research conducted in Côte d'Ivoire, Morocco, and Niger under the supervision of Sylvaine Lemeilleur, Max Rousseau, Frédéric Lançon, Paule Moustier, Lou D'Angelo, Mohammed Aderghal, Eduardo Brisson, Antoine Boyet, Bruno Romagny, and Tarik Harroud.

The research program and this volume draw on a broad series of workshops conducted from 2014 to 2019 at Agence française de développement (AFD) headquarters in Paris. Entitled "Rethinking the Role of Markets," the series was initiated by Gaëlle Henry and Marjolaine Cour and produced by Gaëlle Balineau, Nicole Madariaga, Alix Françoise, and Jean-René Cuzon, with the active involvement of François Giraudy, Florence Mouton, Irène Salenson, and Claude Torre.

The research program could not have taken place without assistance from Cyrille Bellier, Marie Bjorson-Langen, Vincent Caupin, Karine de Frémont, Hélène Djoufelkit, Gilles Kleitz, and Anne Odic at AFD headquarters; from Bruno Leclerc, Olivier Pannetier, and Christelle Josselin for the Côte d'Ivoire case; from Eric Baulard, Anne Sophie Kervella, and Caroline Abt for the Morocco case; and from Phillipe Renault, Habibou Boubacar, and Laureline Triby for the Niger case. The authors thank Thomas Mélonio, Sophie Chauvin, Christoph Haushofer, Alain Joly, Ibtissam Qaddi, and Françoise Tiffoin for their copy-editing and prepublication support of the original French version. They also extend thanks to Suzan Nolan and BlueSky International for this meticulous translation into English.

The authors particularly wish to thank everyone who enhanced their thinking through participation in meetings and workshops: Thomas Allen, Sabrina Archambault, Christine Aubry, Pierre-Arnaud Barthel, Laure de Biasi,

Céline Bignebat, Antoine Boyet, Nicolas Bricas, Xavier Brusseau, Laure Criqui, Anne-Cecile Daniel, Clémentine Dardy, Etienne David, Marie-Jo Demante, Charlotte Durand, Roxane Fages, Nicolas Faugère, Jean-Luc François, Karine Frouin, Sylvanie Godillon, Guillaume Graff, Cyriaque Hattemer, Philipp Heinrigs, Raphael Jozan, Gauthier Kholer, Karine Lagarde, Clément Larrue, William Le Bec, Nicolas Le Guen, Juliette Le Pannerer, Laurent Levard, Simona Logreco, Guillaume Meric, Benjamin Michelon, Alexandra Monteiro, Chloé Pinty, Justine Plourde Dehaumont, François Poisbeau, Gwenaelle Raton, Corinne Ropital, Sandra Rullière, Thomas Sanchez, Marie-Hélène Schwoob, Alexis Sierra, Guillaume Soullier, Sébastien Subsol, Marie-Cécile Thirion, Cédric Touquet, Hélène Vidon, Claire Vige Hélie, Laurence Wilhem, Claire Zanuso, and Pauline Zeiger.

The authors also acknowledge the invaluable contributions made to this volume by anonymous reviewers.

About the Authors

Gaëlle Balineau

Gaëlle Balineau, a development economist, was appointed Agence française de développement (AFD) Regional Project Manager for East Africa in 2019, based in Nairobi, Kenya. She joined AFD in 2014, coordinating research programs on food chain production, quality, structure, trade, and industrialization. Prior to joining AFD, Balineau worked as a consultant for the World Bank on trade assistance projects in Cameroon and Lesotho and as a consultant for Barry Callebaut, a Swiss chocolate manufacturer, researching Ivorian cocoa plantation economic and environmental sustainability. Balineau holds a doctorate in development economics from the University of Clermont-Auvergne Center for Studies and Research on International Development (CERDI). Her doctoral dissertation analyzed the effects of fair trade cotton in Mali and fair trade consumption systems in France. Balineau has long focused on the intersection of food market regulation and fair and sustainable development.

Arthur Bauer

Arthur Bauer, an economist, currently works for the French Treasury General Directorate, where he helps to develop France's macroprudential policy and contributes to the public policy dialogue on debt and household finance. Bauer also studies the effects of formal business tax optimization on fiscal revenue and business income tax growth in Senegal. Previously, he worked with AFD on research to identify entrepreneurial qualities in young people, for Evaluation for Policy Design to assess a microfinance program in Thanjavur (India), and for the World Bank as a consultant on sustainable land management practices. Bauer, a graduate of École Nationale de la Statistique et de l'Administration Économique (ENSAE) ParisTech, holds a master's degree in public administration in international development from the Harvard Kennedy School and is completing a doctoral dissertation in economics at the Centre de Recherche en Économie et Statistique (CREST).

Martin Kessler

Martin Kessler, an economist, works on development policies. As a consultant for the World Bank, he coauthored reports on growth and competitiveness in Myanmar and contributed to building the capacity of its Central Statistical Office and Finance Ministry. Kessler has worked for the Reserve Bank of India, for several African countries as a development strategy consultant, and for the Peterson Institute for International Economics as a researcher, publishing reports on "hyperglobalization," China's emergence, and China's effect on world trade and the financial system. Kessler began his career at the French Embassy in Berlin as an economic attaché and worked for Bruegel, a European think tank, as an analyst. He holds master's degrees from the Paris School of Economics and the Harvard Kennedy School.

Nicole Madariaga

Nicole Madariaga, an economist, was appointed head of the AFD Local Finance and Decentralization Team in the Urban Development, Planning and Housing Department in 2019. She had joined the department in 2014 as an economist for several knowledge production projects on subjects including urban food, jobs, and climate resilience. She first joined AFD in 2010, working in the Macroeconomic Analysis and Country Risk Department. Prior to joining AFD, Madariaga worked for the French Treasury and Economic Policy General Directorate as an international business and trade analyst. She holds a doctorate in economics from the University of Paris I Panthéon-Sorbonne. Her dissertation focused on trade integration, industrial activity location, and regional economic convergence in Latin America. Madariaga has also taught courses in international trade, development economics, and spatial economics at University of Paris I, École Nationale de la Statistique et de l'Administration Économique (ENSAE), and an engineering school.

Abbreviations

AFD	Agence française de développement
ANOPACI	Association nationale des organisations professionnelles agricoles de Côte d'Ivoire (National Association of Professional Agricultural Organizations of Côte d'Ivoire)
CEPII	Centre d'études prospectives et d'informations internationales (Center for International Outlook Studies and Information)
ECAM	Enquête camerounaise auprès des ménages (Center for International Outlook Studies and Information)
FAO	Food and Agriculture Organization (of the United Nations)
GDP	gross domestic product
ICT	information and communications technologies
ITU	International Telecommunication Union
MIS	market information system
OCPV	Office d'aide à la commercialisation des produits vivriers de Côte d'Ivoire (Food Products Marketing Office of Côte d'Ivoire)
OECD	Organisation for Economic Co-operation and Development
ONSSA	Office national de sécurité sanitaire des produits alimentaires (National Office for the Sanitary Safety of Food Products)
OPVN	Office des produits vivriers du niger (Nigerien Food Products Office)
PPP	public-private partnership
RECA	Réseau national des chambres d'agriculture du Niger (National Network of Chambers of Agriculture)
SDG	Sustainable Development Goal
SNEM	Société nouvelle d'exploitation de marque (New Brand Operating Company)
VIP	village information point

Overview

Context: Food Supply and Distribution Infrastructure: The Heart of the UN Sustainable Development Goals (SDGs)

Sustainable Food Systems: A Necessary Condition for Achieving the SDGs

Food systems encompass the entire range of actors and their interlinked value-adding activities for the production, aggregation, processing, distribution, consumption, and disposal of food products that originate from agriculture, forestry, or fisheries (FAO 2018). A food system is composed of several sub-systems, such as an agricultural finance system or irrigation system, and it interacts with other systems, such as health care, commerce, and education. A sustainable food system delivers food security and nutrition for all in such a way that the economic, social, and environmental bases to generate food security and nutrition for future generations are not compromised (FAO 2018).

In recent decades, profound changes have affected food systems, including demographic changes such as rapid population growth and urbanization; economic and social changes such as a rise in inequalities, poverty, trade globalization, and a middle class in developing countries; technological changes such as expanded use of robots and information and communications technology (ICT); as well as climatic changes and natural resource depletion. As a result, taking steps to improve food system sustainability is essential to achieving several SDGs. First, to fight food insecurity and malnutrition, sustainable food systems must adapt to these changes, particularly in urban areas:

- Globally, hunger is gaining ground (FAO et al. 2018). In 2017, 11 percent of the global population suffered from nutritional deficiencies, with the number of undernourished rising since 2014, reaching 821 million in 2017—that is,

1

one out of nine persons. The situation in Sub-Saharan Africa has deterio-
rated the most: between 2010 and 2017 the percentage of Sub-Saharan
Africans with nutritional deficiencies rose from 19.1 percent to 20.4 percent.
Even North Africa saw an increase, from 5 percent to 8.5 percent.

- Food and nutrition insecurity, always more significant in rural areas, is rising
  in cities from extremely fast urbanization and population growth. Africa and
  Asia will see 90 percent of all urban growth by 2050, adding about 2.5 billion
  more urban dwellers (United Nations 2015). Impoverishment accompanies
  this urban population growth (Ravallion, Chen, and Sangraula 2007), automatically amplifying food insecurity in cities. On average, food purchases
  consume 44 percent of urban household spending in Africa, reaching 53
  percent in Niger (FAO 2018).

- The prevalence of undernutrition, overnutrition, and obesity is growing
  rapidly in urban areas. Although the proportion of children suffering from
  stunting has fallen in rural areas, in urban areas it has risen: one in three
  stunted children now live in cities (IFPRI 2017). Overnutrition and obesity
  have also become more prevalent.

→ By providing good nutrition, sustainable food systems help achieve SDG 1
(end poverty), SDG 2 (fight hunger), and SDG 3 (ensure healthy lives).

Second, the food economy could form the cornerstone of a structural
transformation. Propelled by the growth of populations, urban residents,
and incomes, the food economy already represents a substantial market in
Africa—one expected to reach $1 trillion by 2030 (Byerlee et al. 2013). Growth
in consumer demand for foodstuff volume, variety, and quality could create
opportunities for farmers to raise their incomes, while rural nonfarm workers
involved in upstream and downstream production, particularly distribution,
could also see income gains. Africa's domestic market for agricultural products
remains much larger than its export market, and consumer preferences do not
always shift in favor of imported products (Bricas, Tchamda, and Mouton 2016).
On average in West Africa,[1] imports account for only 8 percent of total food
expenditures. Local farmers supply a large share of the food consumed (Allen
and Heinrigs 2016).

These opportunities for structural transformation are particularly important
to seize in Africa because food processing jobs, often highly local, are largely
resistant to globalization and thus provide sustainable sources of employment
and stable income. In West Africa, the food economy generates 66 percent
of all jobs and will remain the largest source of employment in coming years.[2]
The nonagricultural food sector—manufacturing, processing, transport, and
trade—accounts for 22 percent of food economy jobs and 37 percent of
women's employment. This transfer of labor from the agricultural to the

nonagricultural sector will likely increase as domestic demand grows and changes. For example, in Niger and Nigeria the food processing sector already accounts for half of all manufacturing jobs. In many Sub-Saharan African countries, where youth ages 15–24 represent an estimated 60 percent of the self-employed, the nonagricultural food sector could act as the cornerstone of an imperative political and economic structural transformation. Often less tradable at long distance, these jobs are largely resistant to globalization and therefore are a lasting source of employment and stable income.

→ By providing social and economic benefits, sustainable food systems help achieve SDG 1 (end poverty), SDG 8 (full employment and decent work for all), and SDG 10 (reduce inequalities).

Third, sustainable food systems lie at the heart of territorial, environmental, and climatic challenges. The literature has highlighted the effect of food systems on climate change and natural resources, and vice versa. Climate change creates many food-related vulnerabilities (Paloviita and Jarvela 2015; Vermeulen, Campbell, and Ingram 2012), including declines in nutritional quality; soil erosion; soil, air, and water pollution; and soil and water salinization. These issues and the issue of food waste require changes in agricultural practices and consumption modes. Food system infrastructure also structures space for other productive activities (Desmet and Rossi-Hansberg 2014), thereby helping with other sustainable development challenges such as balancing urban and rural development and reducing urban congestion.

→ By affecting territorial and environmental issues, sustainable food systems help achieve SDG 11 (sustainable cities and communities), SDG 12 (responsible consumption and production), and SDGs 13, 14, and 15 (combat climate change, protect and restore terrestrial and marine ecosystems, halt biodiversity loss).

The Role of Food Supply and Distribution Infrastructure in Improving Food System Sustainability

Market infrastructure for food supply and distribution can serve as an important lever for improving food system sustainability. The term *market infrastructure* encompasses the food system's physical and institutional infrastructure that links farmers to consumers (figure 1.1). It includes any infrastructure that physically or contractually brings supply and demand together. Physical market infrastructure includes urban markets, storage units, consolidation areas, retailers, wholesale markets, supermarkets, and shippers. Institutional market infrastructure includes quality standards, ICT and price information systems, contracts, purchasing processes, competition rules, and national and international regulations. In the following ways, market infrastructure has an important impact on how food systems function and therefore on achieving the SDGs:

- Most simply, market infrastructure makes trade possible. Trade is impossible in the absence of physical and contractual infrastructure that brings supply and demand together (Calmette, forthcoming).
- Market infrastructure directly affects consumer and producer food prices. Because food prices are high in Africa compared with those in other regions and with the prices of nonfood goods, low purchasing power limits households' access to foodstuffs of sufficient quality and quantity (Allen 2017). Improvements in market infrastructure affect prices by, for example, reducing transport costs, improving logistics, increasing competition, regulating monopolies, and achieving economies of scale (Quattri 2012).
- Market infrastructure affects farming's physical spaces, producer and consumer market access, and regional development balance. Policy interventions that affect the market infrastructure for price formation for goods and land influence where activities will be located, affecting in turn transport distances and creating spillover effects on farmland (Fafchamps and Hill 2005) and regional development (Calmette, forthcoming; Calmette and Bontems, forthcoming; Straub 2019).
- Market infrastructure determines the quality of food through storage facilities, logistics, cold chain maintenance, quality inspections, and so forth, particularly in localities where quality control regulation takes a back seat to food security and nutrition (Lemeilleur, D'Angelo, et al. 2019).
- Market infrastructure can reduce food losses, thereby improving food system sustainability and lowering food prices. All forms of food losses represent about a third of production (FAO 2017), or 150 kilograms per capita per year in Sub-Saharan Africa, and more than 200 kilograms per capita per year in North Africa (FAO 2020). Unlike in developed countries, in Sub-Saharan Africa the vast majority of food losses occur prior to consumer purchase. For example, 35–45 percent of fruit and vegetable production is lost during their harvest (10 percent), processing (25 percent), and distribution (10 percent). Therefore, even marginal gains in food system efficiency and food waste reduction could have major effects on producers and consumers.

Although market infrastructure plays an essential role in food system sustainability and therefore achievement of the SDGs, research and public development policy have largely underestimated its importance, particularly in Africa, with serious consequences because supply and demand have greatly changed in recent decades. These changes call for a new approach to market infrastructure.

Rethinking Market Infrastructure in Order to Design Sustainable Food System Policies

The Big Gap Separating Newly Identified Needs and Planned Market Infrastructure Projects

Substantial changes have directly and indirectly affected food supply and distribution infrastructure. The changes just mentioned, such as urbanization, trade globalization, technology utilization, and climatic effects, have transformed the food economy (Reardon, Bereuter, and Glickman 2016) and its infrastructure needs. Consequently, supermarkets have emerged (Reardon, Timmer, and Minten 2012; Weatherspoon and Reardon 2003), and the rapid diffusion of technology has had many other impacts (Lemeilleur, Aderghal, et al. 2019). For example, many farmers, wholesalers, shippers, retailers, and consumers now use mobile phones to access information about prices, volume, and quality, even in the remotest rural areas (Aker and Mbiti 2010). Freezers and refrigerated trucks have played a key role in extending supply chains. Far-reaching changes in the way global value chains function have affected farmers, giving them direct access to markets. They have also changed production locations and client–supplier contractual relationships (Lemeilleur, Aderghal, et al., 2019; Lemeilleur, D'Angelo, et al. 2019; World Bank 2020). In this context, food system sustainability seems unimaginable without food supply and distribution infrastructure undergoing a major renewal.

And yet market infrastructure has only slowly changed in response to the growth of African cities because they are hampered by three major characteristics (Lall, Henderson, and Venables 2017). First, the cities lack density: residents often live in unplanned, informal neighborhoods near places of business. Second, they lack scale effects: African cities are often a collection of neighborhoods having little connection to a coherent whole. And, third, they are expensive: the cost of living and doing business is 30 percent higher than in other regions (Nakamura et al. 2016). As a result, African cities see only a weak correlation between urbanization and wealth generation unlike cities in other parts of the world. Meanwhile, they remain relatively unproductive because they have urbanized without industrializing (Gollin, Jedwab, and Vollrath 2016). Furthermore, the lack of private or public investment in high-quality physical and institutional infrastructure has led to economic losses in all sectors, including agriculture and food.

The importance of designing urban food policies and taking a multisectoral approach has only recently dawned on policy makers. Improving market infrastructure requires a multisectoral approach that comprises urban planning, transport and logistics, waste management, rural development, food processing, vocational training, finance, and so forth. Alongside national governments, municipalities and rural communities have a role to play in this new approach (AFD 2017). The 2015 Milan Urban Food Policy Pact, adopted by 163 municipalities worldwide, attests to policy makers' recent gains in awareness because, by signing the pact, they have committed to supporting sustainable agricultural and food systems.[3] However, market infrastructure improvement projects rarely stem from a comprehensive plan. Scattered governance responsibilities for market infrastructure stymie a comprehensive approach. For example, municipal governments oversee retail markets and intraurban transport; some rural localities cover storage infrastructure; national governments control wholesale markets and national transport; and the private sector increasingly takes care of logistics and distribution.

Furthermore, donors and technical assistance providers do not sufficiently integrate their offerings. Several technical and financial partners, international institutions, and researchers support this observation. All conclude that providers must (1) move from a production-centric approach to a holistic one that integrates supply, demand, and market infrastructure; (2) place greater emphasis on the institutional, policy, and governance developments prompted by the larger engagement of local governments, businesses, and civil society in urban food issues; (3) focus more on demand and therefore on the downstream s ide of agricultural and food processing systems, particularly their urban dimensions; and (4) take a multisectoral approach (IFAD 2017; IFPRI 2017; Tefft et al. 2017). And yet the food crisis of 2007–08 has strongly influenced the strategies and recommendations of AFD partners and peers. Since 2009, their discussions and the literature have focused more on price volatility, regulation, food crisis prevention, early warning systems, and how to protect the poorest consumers and farmers from price shocks.

This Volume's Analytical Approach

Updating the Literature
Gaps in research and studies also hinder the development of a new approach to thinking about market infrastructure. On the one hand, the vast majority of research efforts have historically focused on improving agricultural productivity. On the other hand, after the 2007–08 food crisis, researchers, governments, and development organizations shifted their attention to crisis prevention and management, reducing efforts to improve normal, noncrisis food system operations.

The literature on agricultural and food systems and the infrastructure of such systems dates back to the 1970s, when economists studying African subsistence food markets emphasized the need for effective marketing—a system that could convey consumers' needs to producers and increase the latter's ability to react to market signals. Economists thought that by disseminating information and establishing wholesale markets, price competition would automatically prompt production and demand adjustments. Geographers, having a less mechanical view of the situation, accurately described marketing channels for urban markets. For example, research in Central Africa has shown a geographic polarization between cities and the hinterlands—city dwellers' food supply depends on distant inputs, leading to supply difficulties and more long-distance transport. Finally, spatial economics studies have begun to show that product perishability and transport constraints determine urban food supply flows, with the most perishable products provided by areas nearest to the city. Many economists emphasize the role of intermediaries and the institutional trade environment (see Lemeilleur, D'Angelo, et al. 2019 for a literature review).

The literature has been updated recently, but it remains limited, especially for Africa. Much research has been conducted on the "supermarket revolution" (Reardon et al. 2009). However, these studies mainly look at Asia, which has seen the biggest changes. In North Africa, studies mainly take an upstream production-oriented approach, more rarely analyzing downstream urban or spatial factors. In Sub-Saharan Africa, some studies examine the question of whether supermarkets are gaining on the still-prevalent traditional markets, but such studies mainly concern East Africa. A lack of data and indicators contributes to these shortcomings, as does a lack of analysis of the noneconomic social, political, historical, and cultural functions of markets. Geographical economics, urban economics, and urbanism provide useful approaches to studying market infrastructure by analyzing the location, competition, and spatial structuring of food production and consumption. Some studies focus on food deserts (Weatherspoon et al. 2013, 2015; Wrigley et al. 2002). However, such research is limited to Organisation for Economic Co-operation and Development (OECD) countries. Studies of decentralization and public finance examine how decentralization influences public services delivery (Caldeira and Rota-Graziosi 2014; Caldeira, Rota-Graziosi, and Foucault 2012), but these studies barely, if at all, cover commercial infrastructure services, particularly because local authorities rarely consider such infrastructure a public service.

Other areas of inquiry that call for analysis and study include political economies, infrastructure management modes, community relations, merchant associations, private sector actors, tax collection methods, and the influence of these areas on efficiency (Michelon 2008). The diffusion of information about food markets is extremely important (see Bignebat, Koç, and Lemeilleur 2009, on Turkey). Several studies analyze how new information and communications technology makes markets more efficient by improving information flows, thereby reducing some actors' transfer costs or market power. However, these studies generally concentrate on the producer end of the food value chain (Aker 2008; Jensen 2007). This volume aims to close some of these research gaps and to provide development practitioners with an analytical approach they can apply when designing policies to improve food systems in general and market infrastructure in particular.

Methodology: An Analytical Approach Using Three West African Cities as Case Studies

Because the cross-cutting nature of food systems and market infrastructure calls for using several disciplines and tools to inform operational policy recommendations, this volume is based on case studies of three cities: Abidjan in Côte d'Ivoire; Rabat-Salé-Témara in Morocco,[4] and Niamey in Niger. To assemble these case studies, researchers collected quantitative and qualitative data on urban markets by conducting numerous surveys of consumers and intermediaries and by conducting a cartographic survey, visiting retail and wholesale markets, and following up on specific food product sectors to gain detailed pictures of actors and infrastructure. The three cities present different geographical locations and income levels, making it possible to highlight common features and important differences—all useful for informing public policies.[5] As a complement to these cases, this volume draws on a review of geographical economics and urban economics literature for its theoretical framework (Calmette, forthcoming).

Organization of This Volume

Chapter 1 describes the challenges of improving food system sustainability via market infrastructure. Chapter 2 then focuses on physical infrastructure, and chapter 3 on market institutions, as illustrated in figure O.1.

Principal Findings

The Role of Physical Market Infrastructure in Connecting Farmers to Urban Consumers and Shaping Regions

In Côte d'Ivoire, Morocco, and Niger, farms have moved away from cities as centrifugal forces have overtaken centralizing forces (figure O.2). Centrifugal forces include urbanization, which increases the cost of land, and globalization, which makes international markets more attractive than domestic ones, encouraging the move toward larger farms to scale returns and make specific investments. Centralizing forces, such as transport costs and product perishability, tend to bring farms closer to cities. Such forces usually diminish as a country's development level rises. Thus centralizing forces are weaker in Rabat than in Niamey.

The situation differs by country and degree of product perishability. Production takes place farther from Rabat than from Abidjan or Niamey, where some food sectors—often the most perishable vegetable, fruits, and animal

Figure 0.1 Organization of This Volume

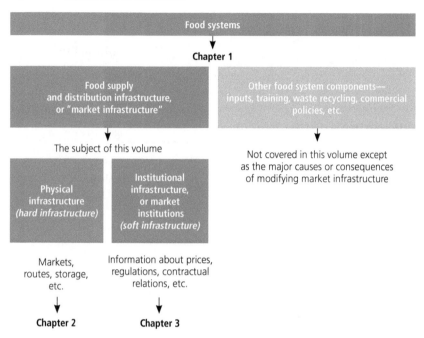

Source: AFD study team.

Note: In this volume, the market institutions under review include more components than are usually covered by the term *soft infrastructure.*

products—remain urban or have declined only in suburban areas. For less perishable vegetables or in countries that have better cold chain technology, food products can be shipped in from more distant areas or imported. Grain products are generally produced in medium-distance regions in each country, or in neighboring countries for Niamey in Niger, which shares borders with four other countries. Rice and frozen products are often imported, provided that the latter can remain within an unbroken cold chain.

More intermediaries and infrastructure are needed when the place of product origin is farther away. The first intermediary is the so-called trader-collector driver who collects products from farmers. These drivers bring products to a wholesaler that negotiates and trades in large volumes. The wholesaler then sells smaller volumes of products to distributors and retailers that in turn sell their products to consumers. Distance increases transport costs and either lowers the intermediary's margins or increases consumer prices when such costs are passed on.

The availability of infrastructure that connects producers to marketplaces varies greatly from city to city. In Rabat, a law requires the use of wholesale markets for fruits and vegetables. Abidjan does not have a designated wholesale marketplace; instead, large open-air markets in the city center perform this function more informally. Niamey also has informal central markets—the Grand Marché and the Katako Market centralize wholesale transactions and also feature retailer sellers. Wholesale marketplaces are thought to improve product allocation and price discovery efficiency. However, municipal authorities use them as a fiscal resource, sometimes to the detriment of the wholesale marketplaces because taxing them encourages the development of informal, untaxed marketplaces.

Figure 0.2 **Centrifugal and Centralizing Forces Affecting Farms: Côte d'Ivoire, Morocco, and Niger**

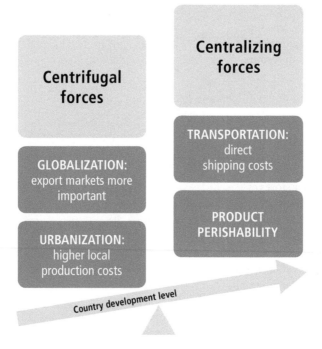

Source: AFD study team.
Note: Centralizing forces diminish as a country's development level rises.

Consumers factor product price, quality, variety, and travel costs into their choice of marketplace. Their most stringent criteria depend on household and city characteristics. For example, proximity is the predominant criterion of consumers in Abidjan, a highly congested, complex city shaped around a lagoon and inlets, whereas price remains the decisive criterion in Niamey. Only Rabat sees consumer concerns about quality beginning to emerge.

Distributors make strategic choices about market location and product price, quantity, and variety, depending on consumer demand, transport costs, and competition. Consumers, subject to the market power of distributors, will be more or less captive, depending on the distributors' choice of location and possible regulation by public authorities. It is desirable to prevent situations in which the poorest people pay more because they must purchase food close to home—a situation often observed in the literature (Calmette, forthcoming). A single marketplace generally allows more competition, but forces buyers to bear travel costs. Conversely, dispersed marketplaces increase distributors' market power and can increase consumer prices.

Retail markets, supermarkets, convenience stores, and microretailers coexist in complementary roles. Microretailers (street vendors and peddlers), who are often the main resource in the poorest or remotest neighborhoods, source products from open-air unloading areas. Meanwhile, supermarkets are playing a growing role in developing countries (Reardon et al. 2003), but they remain limited in West Africa. They improve product quality and lower costs by integrating the supply chain, but they are usually located in wealthier neighborhoods or are accessible only by car, as in Rabat. However, this situation, too, is changing—for example, discount supermarkets are expanding in Abidjan. Despite the growth of supermarkets, the vast majority of consumers favor smaller stores or informal sellers. Thus policies that reduce small retailers' operating costs are essential, even in a city like Rabat, where microretailers remain important in the poorest neighborhoods.

Goals for Policy Makers?
Transport is an integral part of food policy. In the short term, subsidizing transport costs can be an effective policy in cities where supply is elastic. In the medium term, some types of infrastructure can significantly affect prices. For example, often retail markets have facilities that do not maintain the cold chain, thereby increasing costs and lowering food quality. In particular, countries affected by strong seasonal variations in availability can see less price volatility—and therefore less food insecurity—from improved transport and storage infrastructure. Policy makers can also encourage food processing, including canning (the simplest form), in order to provide manufacturing jobs, diversify product offerings, and extend product shelf life, particularly for vegetables.

However, hybrid or fragmented governance and a lack of human or financial resources can threaten the effectiveness of these kinds of policies. The governance of food systems in general and food market infrastructure in particular overlaps three levels of government:

- At the national level, food system governance is shared by three ministries: the Ministry of Agriculture is in charge of agricultural production, including health issues; the Ministry of Trade is often responsible for wholesale markets and international trade; and the Ministry of Transport or Construction is responsible for all physical infrastructure. Food distribution issues are not necessarily central to the missions of these ministries. Furthermore, in Côte d'Ivoire and Niger these ministries lack financial and human resources.

- At the local level, cities regulate retail markets. Since the wave of administrative decentralization in 1980–1990, municipal responsibilities have multiplied without commensurate funding allocations. Their resources often largely depend on levying transaction taxes on the food markets and on leasing spaces to sellers, complicating the relationship between promotion and taxation. Municipalities also determine the nature of crucial public urban transit policies.

- Finally, private business associations and other groups that manage transport, storage, marketplaces, and other infrastructure play an important yet often underestimated role. They frequently form cooperatives that have public-private partnership (PPP) contracts with a municipality, or they create more informal organizations, with members drawn from neighborhood communities. Private groups also determine market rules, infrastructure investments, and daily management. Depending on their power, these private groups may exclude microretailers. Often in the poorest neighborhoods, such groups have only a few stalls and directly compete with informal sellers who offer products from the same sources.

Any food distribution policy intervention must pay attention to potential constraints, such as the role of distance in producer, distributor, and consumer choices; each of these actor's reactions to price changes; product perishability as a factor in location selection; the risk of infrastructure monopolization; and the importance of spatial competition to prevent consumers from becoming captive. Policy makers must also have a fine-tuned understanding of governance issues and broadly consult national, regional, and local stakeholders (including civil society) to hear concerns from all voices.

The Stepchildren of Food Policy: Matching Institutional Market Infrastructure with Supply and Demand

Establishing an Institutional Environment Conducive to Trade

Beyond physical infrastructure, an effective food distribution system relies on other key elements such as access to credit, prices, and information about quality. It also requires trust in institutions and contracts. Chapter 3 in this volume describes the private arrangements and public policies that establish a favorable trade environment at every stage of food production and distribution.

Trade's most fundamental problem emerges in situations in which interactions are sequential—that is, the first party initiates a cooperative exchange, and the second party has an incentive to unilaterally deviate from the proposed cooperation and engage in uncooperative behavior (Greif 2000). Internalizing the second party's incentive, the first party will prefer to not initiate a cooperative exchange.

In the context of food supply and distribution, this problem must be resolved for producer and wholesaler transactions and at all stages of the value chain up to the consumer's purchase. Nevertheless, various parties can remain uncooperative—for example, when sellers have an interest in not revealing the true quality of a product or in overstating the quantity of goods offered. In contrast with the late medieval Maghrebian and Genoese merchants studied by Greif (2000), what he calls "modern" societies developed a cluster of institutions founded on information and contracts. These institutions ensured that contracts were enforced, creating favorable conditions for trade relations to emerge.

In Côte d'Ivoire, Morocco, and Niger, these institutions have a lower than average level of development.[6] Contract enforcement mechanisms are especially weak in markets for services and goods, including food, making the use of contracts quite costly. In the absence of credible contracts, the economic literature shows that trust can create cooperative relationships. This finding explains why individuals from different societies can agree to cooperate. According to Cahuc and Algan (2014), the percentage of a population people believe they can trust affects the level of trade among them. In fact, the larger the percentage of those believed trustworthy, the more a person who wishes to cooperate will expect high gains from cooperating, and thus the more he or she will be inclined to initiate an exchange. Trust levels are particularly low in Morocco and in most of the Sub-Saharan African countries covered by the World Values Survey (Inglehart et al. 2014). This finding is consistent with the well-established relationship between trust levels and per capita income levels.

A lack of trust or contract enforcement mechanisms affects food supply and distribution efficiency by limiting the ability of buyers and sellers to guarantee a transaction or specify its terms. This inability amplifies another barrier to trade—difficulty accessing market information, particularly a product's price–quality equation. Empirically, Côte d'Ivoire, Morocco, and Niger have underdeveloped quality standards for goods and services compared with the rest of the world, and price information remains difficult to obtain. As a result, numerous studies have found significant supply–demand imbalances and suboptimal goods allocation in African food markets, including those in the three countries studied here, especially Niger (Araujo, Araujo-Bonjean, and Brunelin 2012).

Difficulties in accessing credit further hinder the establishment of efficient food distribution systems and trade. Each step in the food value chain, from agricultural production to wholesale and retail distribution, involves entrepreneurial activities that require a properly functioning credit market. However, entrepreneurs and established businesses have more difficulty accessing formal financial services and credit in Côte d'Ivoire, Morocco, and Niger than elsewhere, further constraining the development of their food distribution systems.

Private Arrangements for Facilitating Market Matching

In this institutional context, the private sector has developed arrangements to enable trading in food goods. Private credit, price discovery, and quality assurance arrangements observed in Côte d'Ivoire, Morocco, and Niger address each of the difficulties just identified. To solve fundamental trading problems, food distribution chain intermediaries create informal credit markets and seek market price information, while retailers establish trust with consumers through repeated interactions, allowing product quality to be revealed in the absence of official quality standards. Policy makers must understand the existing arrangements for three factors before considering any public policy intervention—especially "modernization"—that could destabilize the arrangements, thereby reducing trading effectiveness:

- *Access to credit.* In Abidjan, retailers' access to informal credit supports development of the food distribution system. Informal credit arrangements combine punishment mechanisms with repeated interactions that establish a relationship of trust and regularity. In Niger, social proximity—that is, belonging to the same family or the same ethnic group—creates trust and informal credit solutions. In Morocco, private contractual arrangements between suppliers and buyers alleviate farmers' difficulties in accessing credit.

- *Price information.* In all three countries, intermediaries facilitate the acquisition of price information. Although the literature emphasizes the role of ICT in integrating markets and improving goods allocation (Aker and Mbiti 2010), despite widespread mobile phone ownership in Morocco physical intermediaries reduce information costs by aggregating price and quality information for collector-drivers who purchase for retailers. In Niger, intermediaries who facilitate remote transactions are often selected from a trusted network of individuals.

- *Quality assurance.* Trusting relationships are formed to remove uncertainty about quality, overcoming the lack of quality standards. In Morocco, the market for mint, for example, is structured around a network of sellers that maintain trust. Narrow family ties facilitate gaining information about the quality of traded goods. Large stores ensure quality foods through vertical integration such as when marketing tomatoes.

Limitations of These Arrangements

First, the need to establish trust prior to any commercial relationship creates barriers to entry for intermediaries. Indeed, establishing trust from repeated interactions is a time-consuming process. Some trading parties will not spend the time and effort required to set up a commercial relationship with a new entrant because they perceive the cost of doing so as too high. This factor leads to market monopolies or oligopolies in which established reputations override new competitors (Auriol, Balineau, and Bonneton, forthcoming), as observed in wholesale markets in Morocco and Niger.

Second, the reliance of intermediaries on social proximity reduces the number of possible matches, possibly curbing the expansion of some businesses. The exclusion of individuals from the labor market because they do not belong to a certain family or social or economic network also hinders hiring and job creation.

Third, the informal credit market's sometimes usurious interest rates raise the issue of protections for borrowers. A desire to serve a risky loan market and to offer interest rates that make it possible to comply with prudential rules creates a certain tension between lender and borrower. Often, however, interest rates are driven by lenders' market power (Dallimore 2013) rather than by risk premiums.

Finally, the lack of quality standards prevents the vertical differentiation of products sold in supermarkets. It even hinders the development of value-adding processing for some products because consumers, unable to refer to reliable quality standards, overvalue their relationship with trusted sellers when making domestic consumption decisions.

Faced with the many limitations of these private sector arrangements, government interventions have stepped in with solutions, including microfinance support, attempts to regulate quality, and systems to disseminate price information in the markets. For example, microfinance has become significantly more important to the Moroccan economy, but it could play an even greater role with small retailers, enabling them to continue their activities. However, recent studies suggest that offering microloans likely increases competition at various food distribution stages without necessarily resulting in borrowers' economic well-being. The Moroccan government has taken several steps to improve its regulation of quality, creating a food inspection and monitoring agency and developing regulations that govern food-handling conditions. In Niger, government efforts have focused on increasing farmers' awareness of food quality. Finally, new market information systems have allowed many Sub-Saharan African countries to increase the information available about prices.

Crucially, public policies must avoid destabilizing entire trading systems by undertaking so-called modernization interventions without a real understanding of the entire trading system and its private arrangements. After all, regulating monopoly traders, for example, could upend entire trading networks. Furthermore, introducing official quality standards and inspection systems could prove quite expensive unless consumers are prepared to trust them. Or using a different source of credit may be less profitable for suppliers who use vendor financing.

Conclusion

Research reveals a delicate balance among the factors supporting food systems. Producers' and distributors' choice of location and supply strongly affects the ability of households, particularly poor ones, to ensure their food security and nutrition. A public policy intervention that affects one of the key factors—transport costs, product perishability, or competition—can strongly affect immediate food availability. Such interventions also affect national and regional development in the long term through the allocation of productive activity across territories. The fragility of institutions that allow the construction of trustworthy trading relationships should also be considered to avoid destabilizing food systems when attempting to introduce official quality standards and inspections, or when regulating monopolies or informal networks. Policy makers can avoid these pitfalls by carefully analyzing the situation before implementing any intervention and by acknowledging the hybrid and multistakeholder nature of food system governance in general and market infrastructure in particular.

Notes

1. The original French version, produced by Agence française de developpement (AFD), refers to the geographic area discussed in the volume as "West Africa" ("Afrique de l'Ouest"). The World Bank's regional groupings differ in some ways from AFD's, however, and part of the geographic area dealt with in the book would typically be considered part of the Middle East and North Africa region in World Bank publications. For simplicity, however, the English version retains the language of the French original. – Editor.
2. Unless otherwise indicated, the statistics in this paragraph are from Allen, Heinrigs, and Heo (2018).
3. For more information, see the Milan Urban Food Policy Pact, https://www.milanurbanfoodpolicypact.org/.
4. The Morocco case study covers the conurbation of Rabat, Salé, and Témara. For the sake of brevity, this volume refers to the overall urban area as Rabat – Editor.
5. The Côte d'Ivoire case draws on Lançon and Boyer (2019). The Morocco case study draws on Aderghal, Lemeilleur, and Romagny (2019); Lemeilleur, Aderghal, et al. (2019); Rousseau, Boyet, and Harroud (2019); and Rousseau and Harroud (2019). And the Niger case study draws on D'Angelo and Brisson (2019). A summary of the three country case studies can be found in Lemeilleur, D'Angelo, et al. (2019).
6. Greif (2000) uses the World Bank Rule of Law Index to measure these institutions' level of contract enforcement development.

References

Aderghal, M., S. Lemeilleur, and B. Romagny. 2019. "Contribution des systèmes de distribution alimentaire à la sécurité alimentaire des villes: étude de cas sur l'agglomération de Rabat (Maroc)" [The contribution of food distribution systems to urban food security: Case study of Rabat, Morocco]. Notes techniques, No. 48, Agence française de développement, Paris, February. https://www.afd.fr/fr/nt-48-systeme-alimentaire-qualite-sanitaire-aderghal-lemeilleur-romagny.

AFD (Agence française de développement). 2017. "L'AFD et l'alimentation des villes, quel rôle pour les collectivités locales?" [AFD and urban food: What role can local governments play?]. AFD, Paris, September. https://www.afd.fr/fr/lafd-et-l-alimentation-des-villes.

Aker, J. C. 2008. "Does Digital Divide or Provide? The Impact of Cell Phones on Grain Markets in Niger." BREAD Working Paper 177, Bureau for Research and Economic Analysis of Development (BREAD), London School of Economics. http://www.oecd.org/countries/niger/41713177.pdf.

Aker, J. C., and I. M. Mbiti. 2010. "Mobile Phones and Economic Development in Africa." Journal of Economic Perspectives 24 (3): 207–32.

Algan, Y., and P. Cahuc. 2014. "Trust, Well-Being and Growth: New Evidence and Policy Implications." In Handbook of Economic Growth, edited by P. Aghion and S. N. Durlauf, 49–120. Amsterdam: Elsevier Science.

Allen T. 2017. "Le coût des prix alimentaires élevés en Afrique de l'Ouest" [The cost of high food prices in West Africa]. Notes ouest-africaines, No. 8, Organisation for Economic Co-operation and Development, Paris.

Allen, T., and P. Heinrigs. 2016. "Les nouvelles opportunités de l'économie alimentaire ouest-africaine" [New opportunities for the West African food economy]. Notes ouest-africaines, No. 1, Organisation for Economic Co-operation and Development, Paris.

Allen, T., P. Heinrigs, and I. Heo. 2018. "Agriculture, alimentation et emploi en Afrique de l'Ouest" [Agriculture, food, and employment in West Africa]. Notes ouest-africaines, No. 14, Organisation for Economic Co-operation and Development, Paris.

Araujo, C., C. Araujo-Bonjean, and S. Brunelin. 2012. "Alert at Maradi: Preventing Food Crises by Using Price Signals." *World Development* 40 (9): 1882–94.

Auriol, A., G. Balineau, and N. Bonneton. Forthcoming. "The Economics of Quality in Developing Countries in a Global Value Chains World."

Bignebat, C., A. A. Koç, and S. Lemeilleur. 2009. "Small Producers, Supermarkets, and the Role of Intermediaries in Turkey's Fresh Fruit and Vegetable Market." *Agricultural Economics* 40: 807–16.

Bricas, N., C. Tchamda, and F. Mouton, eds. 2016. "L'Afrique à la conquête de son marché alimentaire intérieur: enseignements de dix ans d'enquêtes auprès des ménages d'Afrique de l'Ouest, du Cameroun et du Tchad" [Africa tries to conquer its domestic food market: Lessons from 10 years of household surveys in West Africa, Cameroon, and Chad]. Études de l'AFD, No. 12, 132, Agence française de développement, Paris. https://www.afd.fr/fr/lafrique-la-conquete-de-son-marche-alimentaire-interieur -enseignements-de-dix-ans-denquetes-aupres-des-menages-dafrique-de-louest-du -cameroun-et-du-tchad.

Byerlee, D., A. F. Garcia, A. Giertz, and V. Palmade. 2013. *Growing Africa—Unlocking the Potential of Agribusiness: Main Report*. Washington, DC: World Bank. http:// documents.worldbank.org/curated/en/327811467990084951/pdf/756630v10REPLA 0frica0pub03011013web.pdf.

Cahuc, P., and Y. Algan. 2014. "Trust, Institutions, and Economic Development." In *Handbook of Economic Growth*, Vol. 2A, edited by S. Durlauf and P. Aghion. Oxford, U.K., and San Diego, CA: Elsevier.

Caldeira, E., and G. Rota-Graziosi. 2014. "La décentralisation dans les pays en développement: une revue de la littérature" [Decentralization in developing countries: A review of the literature]. Études et documents, No. 11, CERDI, Paris.

Caldeira, E., G. Rota-Graziosi, and M. Foucault. 2012. "Does Decentralization Facilitate Access to Poverty-Related Services? Evidence from Benin." NBER Working Paper No. 18118, National Bureau for Economic Research, Cambridge, MA.

Calmette, F. Forthcoming. "Le rôle des marchés dans l'approvisionnement alimentaire des villes: un agenda de recherche basé sur la théorie" [The role of markets in urban food supply: A research agenda based on theory]. Papiers de recherche, Agence française de développement, Paris.

Calmette, F., and P. Bontems. Forthcoming. "Infrastructures et territoires" [Infrastructures and territories]. Papiers de recherche, Agence française de développement, Paris.

Dallimore, A. 2013 "Banking on the Poor: Savings, Poverty and Access to Financial Services in Rural South Africa." PhD diss., London School of Economics.

D'Angelo, L., and E. Brisson 2019. "Systèmes d'approvisionnement et de distribution alimentaires: étude de cas sur la ville de Niamey (Niger)" [Food supply and distribution systems: Case study on the city of Niamey, Niger]. Notes techniques, No. 50, Agence française de développement, Paris. https://www.afd.fr/fr/nt-50-marche -alimentation-distribution-groupe8-brisson-emile-geay-dangelo.

Desmet, K., and E. Rossi-Hansberg. 2014. "Spatial Development." *American Economic Review* 104 (4): 1211–43.

Fafchamps, M., and R. V. Hill. 2005. "Selling at the Farm-Gate or Travelling to Market?" *American Journal of Agricultural Economics* 87 (3): 717–34.

FAO (Food and Agriculture Organization of the United Nations). 2017. "The State of Food and Agriculture: Leveraging Food Systems for Inclusive Rural Transformation." Rome. http://www.fao.org/3/a-17658e.pdf.

FAO (Food and Agriculture Organization of the United Nations). 2018. "Sustainable Food Systems: Concept and Framework." Rome. http://www.fao.org/3/ca2079en /CA2079EN.pdf.

FAO (Food and Agriculture Organization of the United Nations). 2020. "SAVE FOOD: Global Initiative on Food Loss and Waste Reduction." Rome. http://www.fao.org /save-food/resources/keyfindings/en/.

FAO (Food and Agriculture Organization of the United Nations), WHO (World Health Organization), IFAD (International Fund for Agricultural Development), WFP (World Food Programme), and UNICEF (United Nations Children's Fund). 2018. "The State of Food Security and Nutrition in the World 2018: Building Climate Resilience for Food Security and Nutrition." FAO, Rome. https://www.who.int/ nutrition/publications/foodsecurity/state-food-security-nutrition-2018-en.pdf.

Gollin, D., R. Jedwab, and D. Vollrath. 2016. "Urbanization with and without Indus- trialization." *Journal of Economic Growth* 21 (1): 35–70.

Greif, A. 2000. "The Fundamental Problem of Exchange: A Research Agenda in Historical Institutional Analysis." *European Review of Economic History* 4 (3): 251–84.

IFAD (International Fund for Agricultural Development). 2017. "Policy Brief— Promoting Integrated and Inclusive Rural-Urban Dynamics and Food Systems." Rome, June. https://www.ifad.org/en/web/knowledge/publication/asset/40256615.

IFPRI (International Food Policy Research Institute). 2017. *Global Food Report 2017.* Washington, DC: IFPRI.

Inglehart, R., C. Haerpfer, A. Moreno, C. Welzel, K. Kizilova, J. Diez-Medrano, M. Lagos, et al., eds. 2014. World Values Survey: Round Six—Country-Pooled Datafile Version. J. D. Systems Institute, Madrid. http://www.worldvaluessurvey.org/WVSDocumentation WV6.jsp.

Jensen, R. 2007. "The Digital Provide: Information (Technology), Market Performance, and Welfare in the South Indian Fisheries Sector." *Quarterly Journal of Economics* 122 (3): 879–924.

Lall, S. V., J. V. Henderson, and A. J. Venables. 2017. *Africa's Cities: Opening Doors to the World*. Washington, DC: World Bank.

Lançon, F., and A. Boyer. 2019. "Contribution des systèmes de distribution alimentaire à la sécurité alimentaire des villes: étude de cas sur l'agglomération d'Abidjan (Côte d'Ivoire)" [The contribution of food distribution systems to urban food security: Case study of Abidjan, Côte d'Ivoire]. Notes techniques, No. 49, Agence française de développement, Paris, February. https://www.afd.fr/fr/nt-49-systeme-alimentaire -urbanisation-abidjan-lancon-boyer.

Lemeilleur, S., M. Aderghal, O. Jenani, A. Binane, M. Berja, Y. Medaoui, and P. Moustier. 2019. "La distance est-elle toujours importante pour organiser l'approvisionnement alimentaire urbain? Le cas de l'agglomération de Rabat" [Is distance always important for urban food supply production? The case of Greater Rabat]. Papiers de recherche, No. 91, Agence française de développement, Paris. https://www.afd.fr/fr/la-distance -est-elle-toujours-importante-pour-organiser-lapprovisionnement-alimentaire -urbain-le-cas-de-lagglomeration-de-rabat.

Lemeilleur, S., L. D'Angelo, M. Rousseau, E. Brisson, A. Boyet, F. Lançon, and P. Moustier. 2019. "Les systèmes de distribution alimentaire dans les pays d'Afrique méditerranéenne et subsaharienne: repenser le rôle des marchés dans l'infrastructure commerciale" [Food distribution systems in Mediterranean and Sub-Saharan African countries: Rethinking the market's role in trade infrastructure]. Notes techniques, No. 51, Agence française de développement, Paris, February. https://www.afd.fr/fr /nt-51-marche-alimentation-distribution-lemeilleur-dangelo-rousseau-brisson-boyet -lancon-moustier.

Maire, B., and F. Delpeuch. 2004. "La transition nutritionnelle, l'alimentation et les villes dans les pays en développement" [The nutritional transition, food, and cities in developing countries]. *Cahiers Agricultures* 13 (1): 23–30.

Michelon, B. 2008. "La gouvernance dans les projets d'équipements marchands en Afrique" [Governance in market facilities projects in Africa]. Paper on occasion of 12th EADI General Conference, "Global Governance for Sustainable Development," Ecole Polytechnique Fédérale de Lausanne, Geneva.

Moustier, P. 2017. "Short Urban Food Chains in Developing Countries: Signs of the Past or of the Future?" *Natures Sciences Sociétés* 25 (1): 7–20.

Nakamura, S., R. Harati, S. Lall, Y. Dikhanov, N. Hamadeh, W. V. Oliver, M. O. Rissanen, and M. Yamanaka. 2016. "Is Living in African Cities Expensive?" Policy Research Working Paper 7641, World Bank, Washington, DC.

Paloviita, A., and M. Jarvela. 2015. *Climate Change Adaptation and Food Supply Chain Management*. London and New York: Routledge.

Quattri, M. 2012. "On Trade Efficiency in the Ethiopian Agricultural Markets." Paper prepared for 123rd EAAE Seminar, Dublin, February 23–24.

Ravallion, M., S. Chen, and P. Sangraula. 2007. "New Evidence on the Urbanization of Global Poverty." *Population and Development Review* 33 (4): 667–701.

Reardon, T., C. B. Barrett, J. A. Berdegué, and J. F. M. Swinnen. 2009. "Agrifood Industry Transformation and Small Farmers in Developing Countries." *World Development* 37 (11): 1717–27.

Reardon, T., D. Bereuter, and D. Glickman. 2016. *Growing Food for Growing Cities: Transforming Food Systems in an Urbanizing World*. Chicago: Chicago Council on Global Affairs.

Reardon, T., C. P. Timmer, C. B. Barrett, and J. Berdegué. 2003. "The Rise of Supermarkets in Africa, Asia, and Latin America." *American Journal of Agricultural Economics* 85 (5): 1140–46.

Reardon, T., C. P. Timmer, and B. Minten. 2012. "Supermarket Revolution in Asia and Emerging Development Strategies to Include Small Farmers." *Proceedings of the National Academy of Sciences* 109 (31): 12332–337.

Rousseau, M., A. Boyet, and T. Harroud. 2019. "Le makhzen et le marché de gros: la politique d'approvisionnement des villes marocaines entre contrôle social et néolibéralisme" [The governing elite and the wholesale market: The supply policy of Moroccan cities straddles social control and neoliberalism]. Papiers de recherche, No. 92, Agence française de développement, Paris. https://www.afd.fr/fr/le-makhzen-et-le-marche
-de-gros-la-politique-dapprovisionnement-des-villes-marocaines-entre-controle
-social-et-neoliberalisme.

Rousseau, M., and T. Harroud. 2019. "Mutation de la gouvernance des systèmes alimentaires urbains: le cas de l'agglomération de Rabat-Salé" [Changes in urban food system governance: The Rabat-Salé case]. Notes techniques, No. 47, Agence française de développement, Paris, February. https://www.afd.fr/fr/nt-47-systeme-alimentaire
-rabat-rousseau-harroud.

Straub, S. 2019. "Transport Infrastructure and the Spatial Evolution of the Productive Structure in Brazil." AFD Research Paper Series, No. 107, Agence française de développement, Paris.

Tefft J. F., M. Jonasova, R. T. O. A. Adjao, and A. M. Morgan. 2017. *Food Systems for an Urbanizing World: Knowledge Product*. Washington, DC: World Bank and Food and Agriculture Organization of the United Nations. http://documents.worldbank.org/curated/en/454961511210702794/Food-systems-for-an-urbanizing-world
-knowledge-product.

United Nations. 2015. *World Urbanization Prospects: The 2014 Revision*. ST/ESA/SER.A/366. UN Department of Economic and Social Affairs, Population Division, New York. https://population.un.org/wup/Publications/Files/WUP2014-Report.pdf.

Vermeulen, S. J., B. M. Campbell, and J. S. Ingram. 2012."Climate Change and Food Systems." *Annual Review of Environment and Resources* 37: 195–222.

Weatherspoon, D., J. Oehmke, A. Dembele, M. Coleman, T. Satimanon, and L. Weatherspoon. 2013. "Price and Expenditure Elasticities for Fresh Fruits in an Urban Food Desert." *Urban Studies* 50 (1): 88–106.

Weatherspoon, D., J. Oehmke, A. Dembele, and L. Weatherspoon. 2015. "Fresh Vegetable Demand Behaviour in an Urban Food Desert." *Urban Studies* 52 (5): 960–79.

Weatherspoon, D., and T. Reardon. 2003. "The Rise of Supermarkets in Africa: Implications for Agrifood Systems and the Rural Poor." *Development Policy Review* (21): 333–55.

World Bank. 2020. *World Development Report 2020: Trading for Development in the Age of Global Value Chains*. Washington, DC: World Bank.

Wrigley, N., D. Warm, B. Margetts, and A. Whelan. 2002. "Assessing the Impact of Improved Retail Access on Diet in a 'Food Desert': A Preliminary Report." *Urban Studies* 39 (11): 2061–82.

Chapter 1

African Cities and Food Systems: Rethinking the Role of Market Infrastructure

Rethinking Food Supply and Distribution Infrastructure to Achieve the UN Sustainable Development Goals (SDGs)

Sustainable Food Systems: A Necessary Condition for Achieving the SDGs

Food systems encompass the entire range of activities involved in the production, aggregation, processing, distribution, consumption, and disposal of food products that originate from agriculture, forestry, or fisheries (FAO 2018). A food system is composed of several subsystems, such as the agricultural finance system or irrigation systems, and interacts with other systems, such as health care, commerce, and education. Figure 1.1 illustrates the components and complexity of the food system. A sustainable food system delivers food security and nutrition for all in such a way that the economic, social, and environmental bases to generate food security and nutrition for future generations are not compromised (FAO 2018).[1]

In recent decades, profound changes have affected food systems, including demographic changes such as rapid population growth and urbanization; economic and social changes, such as a rise in inequalities, poverty, trade globalization, and a middle class in developing countries; technological changes, such as expanded use of information and communications technology (ICT) and robots; as well as climatic changes and natural resource depletion. Indeed, the entire food economy has been modified (Reardon, Bereuter, and Glickman 2016). These recent or upcoming changes pose many new challenges and opportunities. Moreover, improving food system sustainability is essential to achieving several SDGs.

Figure 1.1 **Food System Activities and Actors**

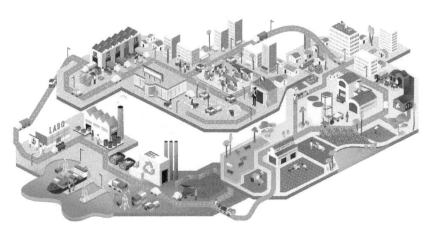

Source: Created for AFD by Planète 7.

Sustainable Food Systems: Indispensable for Combating Food Insecurity and Malnutrition

Globally, hunger is gaining ground (FAO et al. 2018). In 2017, 11 percent of the global population suffered from nutritional deficiencies, an 8 percentage point decrease since 1990 (IFPRI 2017). Despite this progress, the number of under-nourished has risen since 2014, reaching 821 million in 2017, or one out of nine persons. The situation in Sub-Saharan Africa has deteriorated the most; from 2010 to 2017 the percentage of Sub-Saharan Africans with nutritional deficiencies rose from 19.1 percent to 20.4 percent. Even North Africa saw an increase from 5 percent to 8.5 percent from 2010 to 2017. SDG 2, which aims to eradicate hunger and undernutrition in the world by 2030, seems ambitious in light of these recent developments.

Food and nutrition insecurity, always more significant in rural areas, is rising in cities because of extremely fast urbanization and population growth. At present, 40 percent of the poor live in cities in Africa, 47 percent in Asia, and 85 percent in Latin America. Africa and Asia will see 90 percent of all urban growth by 2050, adding about 2.5 billion more urban dwellers (United Nations 2015). Impoverishment accompanies this urban population growth (Ravallion, Chen, and Sangraula 2007), automatically amplifying food insecurity in cities. On average, food purchases consume 44 percent of urban household spending in Africa, reaching 53 percent in Niger (FAO 2018). As of 2007, hunger was more prevalent in cities than in rural areas according to a study of 12 countries by Ahmed et al. (2007).

The prevalence of undernutrition, overnutrition, and obesity is growing rapidly in urban areas. Although the proportion of children suffering from stunting has decreased in rural areas, in urban areas it has increased: one in three stunted children now live in cities (IFPRI 2017). In rural areas, access to food is more problematic and undernutrition is higher than in cities, where overnutrition and obesity are generally far more prevalent. Van Wesenbeeck (2018) draws attention to the complexity of this problem in West Africa, following Bricas (2017), who argues that undernutrition in rural areas most often occurs because of insufficient protein or calorie consumption. In urban areas, undernutrition stems from iron, vitamin A, zinc, and other micronutrient deficiencies that stunt growth.

In West Africa, 110 million people do not have adequate nutrition: 58 million people are malnourished, of which 22 million live in cities and 36 million live in rural areas. An additional 52 million are obese or overweight, the great majority living in urban areas (Van Wesenbeeck 2018). These findings demonstrate that food and nutrition security affects both urban and rural populations. Moreover, because less than a third of food is self-produced, markets and prices are playing a growing role in urban and rural food security issues (Bricas, Tchamda, and Mouton 2016). The final declaration of the 2016 United Nations Conference on Housing and Sustainable Urban Development (Habitat III) recognized food security and nutrition security as two essential needs that should be part of urban development strategies (United Nations 2017).

→ By providing good nutrition, sustainable food systems help achieve SDG 1 (end poverty), SDG 2 (fight hunger), and SDG 3 (ensure healthy lives).

The Food Economy: Cornerstone of a Structural Transformation?

Propelled by the growth of populations, urban residents, and incomes, the food economy already represents a substantial market in Africa—one expected to reach $1 trillion by 2030 (Byerlee et al. 2013). Consumer demand for volume, variety, and quality is also growing. In the West African country of Cameroon and the Central African country of Chad, grains represent less than half of food consumed by value (Bricas, Tchamda, and Mouton 2016). Grains also account for less than 34 percent of food sales in Ethiopia, Mozambique, Tanzania, and Uganda, and only 26 percent in Bangladesh, Indonesia, Nepal, and Vietnam (Reardon, Bereuter, and Glickman 2016). Consumers now want more fruits, vegetables, and other highly perishable fresh produce. They also want milk and meat products, as well as processed and high-value-added foods (Allen, Heinrigs, and Heo 2018).

For higher-income consumers, food quality is increasingly important as they seek freshness, flavor, and specific origins. Particularly in middle-income North African and Asian countries, where the middle classes are emerging and farmers are more reliant on chemical inputs, consumers are changing their purchasing habits to avoid health issues arising from excessive exposure to pesticides (Lançon and Boyer 2019). Growth and changes in demand could create opportunities for farmers to raise their incomes. Rural nonfarm workers involved in up- and downstream production, particularly distribution, could also see income gains. Africa's domestic market for agricultural products remains much larger than its export market, and consumer preferences do not always shift in favor of imported products (Bricas, Tchamda, and Mouton 2016). On average in West Africa, imports account for only 8 percent of total food expenditures, whereas local production accounts for a large share of food consumption (Allen and Heinrigs 2016).

These opportunities for structural transformation are particularly important to seize in Africa because food processing jobs, often highly local, are largely resistant to globalization and thus provide sustainable sources of employment and stable income. In West Africa, the food economy generates 66 percent of all jobs, and it will remain the largest source of employment in the coming years.[2] Beyond the benefits for farmers who may need to increase their productivity and income through new technologies (Choi, Dutz, and Usman 2019), the non-agricultural food sector—manufacturing, processing, transport, and trade—has an enormous potential for job creation. The sector accounts for 22 percent of food economy jobs and 37 percent of women's employment. The transfer of labor from the agricultural to the nonagricultural sector will likely increase as domestic demand grows and changes. For example, in Niger and Nigeria the food processing sector already accounts for half of all manufacturing jobs. In many Sub-Saharan African countries, where youth ages 15–24 represent an estimated 60 percent of self-employed, the nonagricultural food sector could constitute the cornerstone of an imperative political and economic structural transformation.

→ By providing social and economic benefits, sustainable food systems help achieve SDG 1 (end poverty), SDG 8 (full employment and decent work for all), and SDG 10 (reduce inequalities).

Sustainable Food Systems: At the Heart of Territorial, Environmental, and Climatic Challenges

The literature has highlighted the effects of food systems on climate change and natural resources, and vice versa, emphasizing how climate change creates many food-related vulnerabilities (Paloviita and Jarvela 2015; Vermeulen, Campbell, and Ingram 2012). Those vulnerabilities include declines in nutritional quality; soil erosion; soil, air, and water pollution; and soil and water salinization. These issues, and the issue of food waste, require changes in agricultural practices and consumption modes.

Food system infrastructure also structures spaces for other productive activities (Desmet and Rossi-Hansberg 2014), thereby helping with other sustainable development challenges, such as balancing urban and rural development and reducing urban congestion.

Throughout the food chain, food is lost, thrown away, or wasted for technological, economic, and societal reasons. Food waste (unconsumed food) emits 3.3 gigatons of carbon dioxide equivalent per year. Sub-Saharan Africa's food waste averages 210 kilograms of carbon dioxide per person per year—the lowest carbon footprint of any region (see FAO 2013, 2014)—which is equivalent to 87 percent of worldwide road transport emissions. Therefore, developing and improving food storage and processing practices are crucial for limiting the organic and inorganic waste produced by the increased demand for food. This requires policies to reduce overall food waste and to valorize organic food waste (Galannakis 2018).

→ By affecting territorial and environmental issues, sustainable food systems help achieve SDG 11 (sustainable cities and communities), SDG 12 (responsible consumption and production), and SDGs 13, 14, and 15 (combat climate change, protect and restore terrestrial and marine ecosystems, halt biodiversity loss).

The Role of Food Supply and Distribution Infrastructure in Improving Food System Sustainability

This volume argues that market infrastructure for food supply and distribution can serve as an important lever for improving food system sustainability. Moreover, the approach to improving infrastructure needs to be rethought extensively. The term *market infrastructure* encompasses the food system's physical and institutional infrastructure that links farmers to consumers (figure 1.1). It includes any infrastructure that physically or contractually brings supply and demand together. Physical market infrastructure includes urban markets, storage units, consolidation areas, retailers, wholesale markets, supermarkets, and shippers. Institutional market infrastructure includes quality standards, price information systems, contracts, purchasing processes, competition rules, and national and international regulations. In the following ways, market infrastructure has important effects on how food systems function and therefore on achievement of the SDGs:

- Most simply, market infrastructure makes trade possible. Trade is impossible in the absence of physical and contractual infrastructure that brings supply and demand together (Calmette, forthcoming).

- Market infrastructure directly affects consumer and producer food prices. Because food prices are high in Africa compared with those in other regions and the prices of nonfood goods, low purchasing power limits households' access to foodstuffs of sufficient quality and quantity (Allen 2017). Improvements in market infrastructure affect prices by, for example, reducing transport costs, improving logistics, increasing competition, regulating monopolies, and achieving economies of scale (Quattri 2012). Although the effect of market infrastructure on product prices is very difficult to determine prior to implementing a development project or policy, it is nonetheless very important to imagine and plan for contingent effects. For example, a local-level public mobility policy that aims to reduce consumers' cost to access a market by, for example, subsidizing public transit, could prove counterproductive if the measures increase consumer demand without simultaneously increasing supply, resulting in higher prices paid to farmers at the expense of the consumers the mobility policy aimed to help.

- Market infrastructure affects farming's physical spaces, producer and consumer market access, and regional development balance. Policy interventions that affect price formation market infrastructure for goods or land influence where activities will be located, affecting in turn transport distances and creating spillover effects on farmland (Fafchamps and Hill 2005) and regional development (Calmette, forthcoming; Calmette and Bontems, forthcoming; Straub 2019). National and municipal government policies must aim to limit potential congestion, insecurity, and pollution, particularly in urban areas. Policies should also aim to preserve or improve the social, economic, and environmental balance between regions.

- Market infrastructure determines the quality of food through storage facilities, logistics, cold chain maintenance, quality controls, and so forth, particularly in localities where quality control regulation takes a back seat to food security and nutrition (Lemeilleur, D'Angelo, et al. 2019). In urban areas, difficulty accessing healthy foods also contributes to food insecurity (Bricas 2017). Satterthwaite, McGranahan, and Tacoli (2010, cited in Bricas 2017) note that inexpensive restaurants and street food are particularly adapted to the lifestyle of people living in poor urban neighborhoods, accommodating constrained work and commuting schedules and the lack of space in homes. Other scholars emphasize the somewhat unhygienic condition of these food distribution modes and the weak institutional quality control of such markets (Broutin and Bricas 2006, cited in Bricas 2017; Henson 2003). Thus, "while rendering important services by feeding a population that has limited purchasing power, the informal food sector is … often seen as generating health risks for consumers" (Ekanem 1998; Winarno and Allain 1991).

- Market infrastructure can reduce food losses, thereby improving food system sustainability and lowering food prices. All forms of food losses represent about a third of production (FAO 2017), or 150 kilograms per capita per year in Sub-Saharan Africa, and more than 200 kilograms per capita per year in North Africa (FAO 2020). Unlike in developed countries, in Sub-Saharan Africa the vast majority of food losses occur prior to consumer purchase.

For example, 35–45 percent of fruit and vegetable production is lost during their harvest (10 percent), processing (25 percent), and distribution (10 percent). Because the cost of these losses is included in food prices, the losses may both reduce smallholder farmer incomes and increase consumer costs. Therefore, even marginal gains in food system efficiency and food waste reduction could have major effects on producers and consumers.

• Market infrastructure can help all farmers access the market, including smallholders and local producers, while allowing urban and rural consumers to benefit from a variety of quality food at affordable prices. Consumers must be able to satisfy their increasing demand at affordable prices. Farmers must be able to limit the risks associated with ever-changing global supply chains, rapidly expanding supermarkets, and consumers shifting to imports to meet their demand. The "supermarket revolution" (Reardon et al. 2003), like the submerged, unseen part of an iceberg, sees large retail distribution groups negotiating and coordinating trade in a globalized world. This can lead to the exclusion of farmers who are unable to meet the quality, delivery frequency, quantity, and other standards imposed by supermarkets. The physical infrastructure of the market as an institution is essential for smaller and local farmers striving to overcome these challenges.

Although market infrastructure plays an essential role in food system sustainability and therefore in achievement of the SDGs, research and development policy have largely underestimated its importance, particularly in Africa, with serious consequences because supply and demand have greatly changed in recent decades. These changes call for a new approach to market infrastructure.

Rethinking Market Infrastructure in Order to Design Sustainable Food System Policies

The Big Gap Separating Newly Identified Needs and Planned Market Infrastructure Projects

Substantial changes have directly and indirectly affected market infrastructure. The changes just mentioned, such as urbanization, trade globalization, the utilization of technology, and the effects of climate change, have transformed the food economy (Reardon, Bereuter, and Glickman 2016) and its infrastructure needs. Consequently, supermarkets have emerged (Reardon, Timmer, and Minten 2012; Weatherspoon and Reardon 2003), and the rapid diffusion of technology has had many other impacts (Lemeilleur, Aderghal, et al. 2019). For example, many farmers, wholesalers, shippers, retailers, and consumers now use mobile phones to access information about prices, volume, and quality, even in the remotest rural areas (Aker and Mbiti 2010). Freezers and refrigerated trucks have played a key role in extending supply chains. Far-reaching changes in the way global value chains function have affected farmers, giving them direct access to markets. They have also changed production locations and client–supplier contractual relationships (Lemeilleur, Aderghal, et al. 2019; Lemeilleur, D'Angelo, et al. 2019; World Bank 2020a).

Global trade in food products reached $1.5 trillion in 2017, representing 8 percent of world trade. In Sub-Saharan Africa, imports totaled $50 billion, or 15 percent of global imports—twice the value traded 10 years ago (UNCTAD 2017). All regions in Africa have seen enormous increases in formal (documented) exports and imports. However, because many countries cannot police their long land borders, they significantly underestimate the share of informal imports in their food stocks. With the increasing availability of imports, consumer tastes have evolved as have domestic producers' competitors. Logistics needs have changed as well. Global value chains have profoundly changed how food producers, traders, distributors, and retailers coordinate and operate. In the food supply chain, as in other supply chains, the number of suppliers is minimized as centralized purchasing platforms concentrate supplies (World Bank 2020a). Improved rural infrastructure and market liberalization lead to disintermediation as it becomes easier for buyers to access farms and purchase directly from farmers without going through rural intermediaries and as large buyers pursue vertical integration through production and marketing contracts (Lemeilleur, D'Angelo, et al. 2019a).

In this context, food system sustainability seems unimaginable without food supply and distribution infrastructure undergoing a major renewal. And yet market infrastructure has only slowly changed in response to the growth of African cities because they are hampered by three major characteristics (Lall, Henderson, and Venables 2017). First, the cities lack density: residents often live in unplanned, informal neighborhoods near places of business. Second, African cities lack scale effects: they are often a collection of neighborhoods having little connection to a coherent whole. And, third, the cities are expensive: the cost of living and doing business is about 30 percent higher than in other regions (Nakamura et al. 2016). As a result, African cities see only a weak correlation between urbanization and wealth generation unlike cities in other parts of the world. Meanwhile, African cities remain relatively unproductive because they have urbanized without industrializing (Gollin, Jedwab, and Vollrath 2016). Furthermore, lack of private and public investment in high-quality physical and institutional infrastructure has led to economic losses in all sectors, including agriculture and food.

The importance of designing urban food policies and taking a multisectoral approach has only recently dawned on policy makers. Improving market infrastructure requires a multisectoral approach that comprises urban planning, transport and logistics, waste management, rural development, food processing, vocational training, finance, and so forth. Alongside national governments, municipalities and rural communities have a role to play in this new approach (AFD 2017). The 2015 Milan Urban Food Policy Pact, adopted by 163 municipalities worldwide, attests to policy makers' recent greater awareness because, by signing the pact, they have committed to supporting sustainable agricultural and food systems.[3]

However, market infrastructure improvement projects rarely stem from a comprehensive plan because scattered governance responsibilities for market infrastructure stymie such an approach. For example, municipal governments oversee retail markets and intraurban transport; some rural localities cover storage infrastructure; national governments control wholesale markets and national transport; and the private sector is increasingly taking care of logistics and distribution.

Furthermore, donors and providers of technical assistance do not sufficiently integrate their offerings. Several technical and financial partners, international institutions, and researchers support this observation. All conclude that providers must (1) move from a production-centric approach to a holistic one that integrates supply, demand, and market infrastructure; (2) place greater emphasis on the institutional, policy, and governance developments prompted by the increased engagement of local governments, businesses, and civil society in urban food issues; (3) focus more on demand and therefore on the downstream side of agricultural and food processing systems, particularly their urban dimensions; and (4) take a multisectoral approach (IFAD 2017; IFPRI 2017; Tefft et al. 2017). However, the food crisis of 2007–08 has strongly influenced the strategies and recommendations of Agence française de développement (AFD) partners and peers. Since 2009, their discussions and the literature have focused more on price volatility, regulation, food crisis prevention, early warning systems, and how to protect the poorest consumers and farmers from price shocks.

Updating the Literature

Gaps in research and studies also hinder the development of a new approach to thinking about market infrastructure. On one hand, the vast majority of research efforts have historically focused on improving agricultural productivity. On the other, after the 2007–08 food crisis researchers, governments, and development organizations shifted their attention to crisis prevention and management, reducing efforts to improve normal, noncrisis food system operations.

The literature on agricultural and food systems and such systems' infrastructure is dated.[4] Beginning in the 1970s, economists studying African subsistence food markets emphasized the need for effective marketing and a system that could convey consumers' needs to farmers and increase the ability of farmers to react to market signals. Economists thought that by disseminating information and establishing wholesale markets, price competition would automatically prompt adjustments in production and demand (Jones 1972; Timmer, Falcon, and Pearson 1983). Many economists emphasized the role of intermediaries and the institutional trade environment, and studies of food supply in cities in the former Zaire (now the Democratic Republic of Congo) and Côte d'Ivoire followed this logic (Aguié 1997; Goosens, Minten, and Tollens 1994; Tollens 1997). However, many experiments in setting up wholesale markets failed, and market information systems affect only a few actors (Chaléard 1996; Galtier and Egg 2003).

Geographers, taking a more finely grained empirical approach, accurately described marketing channels for urban markets. Vennetier (1972a, 1972b) initiated research in Central Africa, showing geographic polarization between cities and the hinterlands—city dwellers' food supply depends on distant inputs, leading to supply difficulties and more long-distance transport. Chaléard (1996, 1998) showed how much transport constrains locally grown subsistence crops from meeting urban demand. He also showed that food flows between rural and urban areas in both directions, not just one way. He further highlighted the complex way that commercial traders combine a variety of supply and redistribution spaces with a range of products in order to adapt to variable produce delivery times and the geographic distribution of farms. Finally, spatial economics studies inspired by Von Thünen (1826) showed that product perishability and transport constraints determine urban food supply flows, with the most perishable products provided by areas closest to cities, despite the expansion of transport to rural areas and constrained land availability in suburban areas. Geographic proximity often combines with relational proximity between producers and sellers and between sellers and consumers (Moustier 2017).

Economists such as Hugon (1985), Requier-Desjardins (1991), Riley and Staatz (1993), and Harris-White (1996), as well as anthropologists (Guyer 1987), also highlighted the need to describe the chain of intermediaries who operate between farmers and consumers and to clarify their constraints and objectives in order to assess how consumers' food supply might be improved. According to Guyer (1987, 6), "Food distribution systems are not only market chains which ensure the conveyance of goods and the communication of price information, nor merely a link between the classic dyads of analysis, the producer and the consumer, the peasant and the state. They are also organisations rooted in an articulated social and economic structure." Traders are subject to many constraints that are characterized by instability, uncertainty, and variability over time, including product acquisition and sale conditions, financing availability, transport logistics, and information reliability. Trader networks and informal contracts work around these constraints, but the effect of these constraints on overall supply chain efficiency remains poorly understood (Riley and Staatz 1993; Staatz, Dione, and Dembele 1989).

Informal[5] food distribution systems in Africa are often considered ineffective in the face of greater food demand. However, observers also point out such systems remain accessible for underprivileged consumers and prove resilient to supply and demand instability, both of which explain their importance to city dwellers' food supply (Vorley 2013). Some authors have described a modernization of African food systems, defining it as a set of technological and organizational innovations. The latter include changes in the way space is organized, such as grouping product types, achieving economies of scale, and improving logistics. It also covers relationships between actors, such as establishing contractual agreements between producers and buyers, or even vertical integration, which combines different parts of the food value chain, such as when distributors invest in production. Supermarkets are a form of modernization as well, as are wholesale markets equipped with the means to increase product range and price transparency.

Several visions for food system modernization can be found in the literature (Moustier et al. 2009). A positive vision sees modernization as a source of savings, added value, and competitiveness, and as an effective response to the demand for quality. A negative vision emphasizes the risk of exclusion that modernization fuels. A middle path between these two perspectives could show how existing networks could be used rather than replaced through investments in infrastructure, technology, and organizational skills in order to meet the challenges posed by modernization. This volume contributes a detailed empirical description of the constraints to such modernization.

Finally, many studies of urban food governance have been influenced by urban bias theory (Lipton 1977)—that is, authorities prefer to maintain urban social stability through low prices such as by subsidizing imports, a policy that adversely affects rural populations. However, some studies have shown that cities have ripple effects on rural farmers, creating new outlets and intensifying agricultural production (Cour 2004).

Recent Updates to the Literature

The literature has been updated recently, but it remains limited, especially for Africa. Much research has been conducted on the "supermarket revolution" (Reardon et al. 2009). However, these studies mainly focus on Asia, which has seen the biggest changes. In North Africa, studies mainly take an upstream, production-oriented approach, more rarely analyzing downstream urban or spatial factors. In Sub-Saharan Africa, some studies examine whether super-markets are gaining on the still-prevalent traditional markets, but such studies mainly are of East Africa—see, for example, Tschirley et al. (2010) on Zambia and Kenya and Woldu et al. (2013) on Addis Ababa. The following factors explain why the literature for the African continent is limited:

- A lack of data on and indicators for traditional markets (Tschirley et al. 2010), such as location, products distributed, type of ownership and management, purchase price and sales price, and waste
- A lack of data on consumer preferences based on actual purchasing data, such as preferences for places of purchase and the cost and time for transport versus product price (the latter being not the sole variable to consider)
- A lack of analysis of traditional markets' noneconomic social, political, heritage, and cultural functions, which probably helps to explain why it was assumed that supermarkets would sweep away other retailers. This assumption has proved incorrect in Latin America, for example (see Farina 2002)

Geographical economics, urban economics, and urbanism are useful approaches to studying market infrastructure by analyzing location, competition, and spatial structuring of food production and consumption. Some studies focus on food deserts (Weatherspoon et al. 2013, 2015; Wrigley et al. 2002). However, such research is limited to Organisation for Economic Co-operation and Development (OECD) countries. Studies of Sub-Saharan Africa remain rare—see Raton (2012) for an example of a geographical economics approach to Mali. Studies of decentralization and public finance examine how decentralization influences public services delivery (Caldeira and Rota-Graziosi 2014; Caldeira, Rota-Graziosi, and Foucault 2012), but these studies barely, if at all, cover commercial infrastructure services, particularly because local authorities rarely consider such infrastructure a public service and often manage it in partnership with the private sector. Other areas of inquiry that call for analysis and study include political economies, infrastructure management modes, community relations, merchant associations, private sector actors, tax collection methods, and the influence of these areas on efficiency (Michelon 2008).

The diffusion of information on food markets is extremely important (see Bignebat, Koç, and Lemeilleur 2009 on the case of Turkey). Several studies analyze how new information and communications technology makes markets more efficient by improving information flows, thereby reducing some actors' transfer costs or market power. However, these studies generally concentrate on the producer end of the food value chain (Aker 2008; Jensen 2007). This volume aims to fill these research gaps and provide development practitioners with an analytical approach they can apply when designing policies to improve food systems in general and market infrastructure in particular.

Methodology: An Analytical Approach Using Three West African Cities as Case Studies

This volume focuses on how donors and technical assistance providers, such as the World Bank and AFD, can help local and national governments design food policies by (1) focusing on one component of the food system—the food supply and distribution infrastructure—and (2) rethinking the design of food transport, storage, and selling to ensure food and nutrition security for rapidly changing cities, regions, and countries. This rethinking of infrastructure for food policy purposes extends to planning for pollution, ICT utilization, and positive and negative externalities and agglomeration effects. It also looks at how all these elements will affect the location and physical organization of food production, distribution, and sales activities over the long term.

The policies to be designed are multisectoral, transversal, and remarkably complex. Should the creation of wholesale markets be imposed in African countries? If the answer is yes, how can such markets be located close enough to cities to reduce buyers' transport costs, and yet remain distant enough to avoid congesting urban streets and other infrastructure? What rules should govern retail markets, and who should take responsibility for enforcing regulations? Should consumer transportation be subsidized to improve the link between consumers and the market? Is urban agriculture, with its shorter distance between farmer and consumer, more efficient? All food system components are interdependent, from processing to final consumption, making it difficult to solve one problem without taking other problems into account. Furthermore, in recognition of the diverse geographies, actors, and activities, policy makers must take a multidisciplinary approach.

Because the cross-cutting nature of food systems calls for the use of several disciplines and tools to inform operational policy recommendations, this volume relies on case studies. The three cases provide a broader, more descriptive wealth of information than can purely quantitative multicountry comparisons. Furthermore, they account for the complexity of interdependencies among production location, transport and market infrastructure, consumer preferences, and the market power of various players.

The three case studies center on Abidjan in Côte d'Ivoire, Rabat-Salé-Témara in Morocco,[6] and Niamey in Niger. Their different geographies and income levels allow highlighting common features alongside differences, resulting in a wealth of information for policy makers (see box 1.1). Each of the three cities is an administrative or economic capital or both. However, Rabat, unlike the other two cities, is neither the largest city population-wise nor the commercial capital of Morocco. Abidjan, like Rabat, is a port city, which facilitates trade. Meanwhile, each country's ability—or inability—to regulate and enforce regulations also strongly affects the functioning of its markets.

Researchers collected quantitative and qualitative data for the three case studies, focusing on the food supply and distribution infrastructure. Quantitative surveys of consumers and intermediaries covered the following:

- A sample of urban consumers, who were asked about their consumption practices and decision factors for products and retail outlets. Specifically, 312 persons were surveyed in Abidjan; 76 in Rabat, with a focus on hygiene; and 85 in Niamey. The survey samples targeted a variety of socioeconomic profiles in different neighborhoods with contrasting living standards.

- A sample of urban traders, including formal and informal wholesalers and retailers. Eighty-five traders were surveyed in Rabat, including 55 retailers, of which 3 were modern sellers and 31 were wholesalers. In addition, researchers conducted a specific survey of 505 retailers in Rabat about product origin. They also surveyed 67 traders in Abidjan (54 wholesalers and 13 retailers), and 169 traders and 58 shippers in Niamey.

Qualitative research included a cartographic survey, on-site visits to retail and wholesale markets, and follow-ups in specific food product sectors (such as mint) to provide detailed descriptions of the actors and infrastructure. Market governance was studied through interviews with civil servants from the relevant ministries and public and semipublic agencies, elected officials, local technicians, experts, wholesale market managers, large and medium-size distributors, government administrators, politicians, and representatives of civil society, nonprofits, and the private sector. As a complement to these cases, this volume draws on a review of the geographical economics literature for its theoretical framework (Calmette, forthcoming).

BOX 1.1

Sources Consulted for This Volume: A Theoretical Summary and Three Case Studies

This volume is based on a theoretical article and three field studies. All research is available on the AFD website, http://www.afd.fr.

Calmette (forthcoming) has compiled a summary of the findings of geographical economics applied to the question of markets. It provides answers to political economy questions, including: When is it effective, from the policy maker's point of view, to subsidize shipping or transportation costs? Where should a market be located? How will it

(continued next page)

Box 1.1 (continued)

affect farms? The summary reveals that technical constraints, such as product perishability, inform many of the answers, as do consumer preferences for proximity or prices. The summary also reminds the reader that often imperfect—or even monopolistic—market conditions are just as important as physical infrastructure.

Aderghal, Lemeilleur, and Romagny (2019), Lemeilleur, Aderghal, et al. (2019), Rousseau, Boyet, and Harroud (2019), and Rousseau and Harroud (2019) present studies and research on Rabat in Morocco. They describe complex changes in the city's food supply and distribution infrastructure. The primarily geographical changes include distance from farms and whether there is an obligation to use wholesale markets for fruits and vegetables.These changes came about because average consumer incomes increased. However, the changes exclude poorer consumers, sometimes reducing their access to food. Hygiene problems figure prominently. The changes are also social and political: the authors and the Morocco case study highlight the tension between traditional—often informal—distribution circuits made up of micro-retailers, the medina, the souk, and the modern supermarket. The authors describe finely grained changes at the neighborhood level. These studies are based on face-to-face surveys of consumers and producers, geographic and ethnographic descriptions of markets and their spatial contexts, and interviews with political and administrative decision-makers.

Lançon and Boyer (2019) describe a case study of Abidjan, Côte d'Ivoire. They point out that the polycentric configuration of fresh food distribution circuits organized around marketplaces and governed by networks of interpersonal relationships corresponds with the townspeople's preference for proximity. The configuration also responds to the difficulties of moving around the expansive and fragmented agglomeration. Supermarkets remain marginal for the distribution of fresh products. The authors suggest that modernizers of the current little-formalized distribution networks should not aim to concentrate flows around wholesale markets. Instead, modernizers should design deconcentrated and coordinated systems in consultation with traders, sellers, and municipalities. This case study is based on a cartographic analysis, detailed interviews with food sector administrators, and quantitative surveys of consumers and intermediaries in several urban markets.

D'Angelo and Brisson (2019) analyze the case of Niamey in Niger. The context is different from that of Abidjan and Rabat because of major constraints, including supply, production, low incomes, climate risks, weak logistical infrastructure, and low levels of government intervention capacity. Despite all that, the authors emphasize the resilience of the largely informal supply system, which is concentrated in the city center. Because of the landlocked nature of the country, imports (often informal) play a major role. This case study was based on a 2015 report, "An Analysis of the City of Niamey's Commercial Armature" by Groupe Huit and complemented by a 2016 survey of consumers, traders, and shippers. The authors also consulted a synthesis of these three case studies and additional AFD publications on this volume's subject.

Urbanization, Globalization, and Middle-Class Consumers in Côte d'Ivoire, Morocco, and Niger

Population Booms in Ill-Prepared Cities

Like many African countries, Côte d'Ivoire, Morocco, and Niger have experienced sustained population growth in recent decades, by about 10 million each since 1990 (graph 1.1). By 2017, Niger had grown 3.5–4 percent annually to reach 21.5 million inhabitants. And Côte d'Ivoire had grown 2.5 percent per year, close to the Sub-Saharan African average of 2.7 percent per year, to reach 24.3 million. Morocco has a lower birth rate and therefore saw its population increase more slowly, 1.3 percent per year, yet still counted 35.7 million inhabitants by 2017. Graph 1.1 shows population growth trends from 1960 to 2017 in the three countries and in the Sub-Saharan and North African region.

Graph 1.1 **Population Growth in Côte d'Ivoire, Morocco, and Niger Compared with North and Sub-Saharan Africa, 1960–2017**

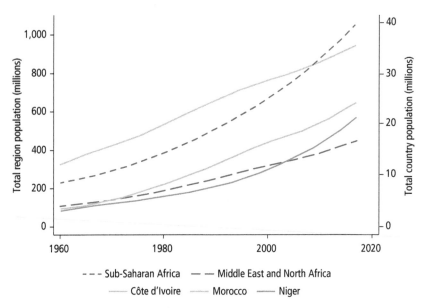

Source: AFD study team, using data from United Nations Statistics Division, Demographic and Social Statistics (database), 2020, https://unstats.un.org/unsd/demographic-social/.

In many African countries, rapid population growth has driven even higher rates of urban population growth, particularly in Côte d'Ivoire and Morocco. Nearly 50 percent of the inhabitants of both countries live in cities. This nearly 10 percentage point increase since 1990 pushes both countries above the nearly 40 percent urban population average of Sub-Saharan Africa. Because Niger's rate of urbanization has remained stable for the past 30 years, it counts only 15 percent of its population as urban, below the regional average. Graph 1.2 illustrates these countries' urban population growth trends since the mid-20th century. In absolute numbers, the rapid increase in urban populations reflects overall population growth.

Graph 1.2 **Urban Population Growth in Côte d'Ivoire, Morocco, and Niger Compared with North and Sub-Saharan Africa, 1960–2017**

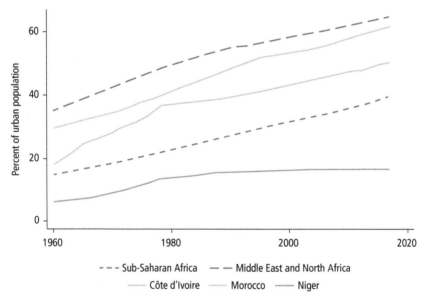

Source: AFD study team, using data from World Bank, World Development Indicators (database), 2020, https://databank.worldbank.org/source/world-development-indicators.

Across the globe, long-established cities and new towns are seeing dynamic population growth. In fact, city dwellers represent more than half of the world's population. Previously distinct urban areas, now more populous than rural areas, have increasingly porous borders, particularly as populations gain mobility. Moreover, urbanization is likely to increase in the future. According to United Nations projections, 2.5 billion people will live in urban areas by

2050 (United Nations 2015). Because 90 percent of this urban population growth will likely occur in African and Asian cities, urbanization will be particularly marked in Africa (United Nations 2015). The new urban lifestyles and consumption habits of these growing urban populations stimulate domestic demand, particularly for foodstuffs.

Cities are ill-prepared to absorb this population growth. The lack of private investment in building construction, public roads, and other facilities creates economic losses in all sectors of activity. For example, paved roads may exist in downtown city centers, but they often disappear as one moves toward the periphery. These shortcomings make it harder for food supply and distribution infrastructure to function in Africa. Retail markets structure the economic, social, and environmental life of a neighborhood, but in Abidjan and Niamey such marketplaces lack easy connections to other infrastructure and prove difficult to maintain, thereby increasing consumer food prices. In Rabat, this problem is relatively limited because of better urban planning.

Urban Food Demand: Increasing, Diversifying, and Carrying Specific Risks

The Growing Demand: A Stimulus for Local Production

A higher demand for food, mainly for local products, accompanies urban population growth. In West Africa, imports account for only 8 percent of total food expenses on average; local farmers supply a large share of the food consumed (Allen and Heinrigs 2016). In Abidjan, for example, despite a significant reliance on imported rice, wheat, fish, milk, and offal, the rapid rise in food demand has strongly mobilized producers in the surrounding countryside (Lançon and Boyer 2019). The Food and Agriculture Organization of the United Nations (FAO) believes that urban food demand could boost rural economies. According to its 2017 *The State of Food and Agriculture* report, "Millions of young people in developing countries who are poised to enter the labor force in the coming decades need not flee rural areas to escape poverty" (FAO 2017). The report also states, "Rural areas actually have vast potential for economic growth pegged to food production and related sectors." In fact, "leveraging growing demand for food in urban areas" will "diversify food systems and generate new economic opportunities in off-farm, agriculture-related activities" (FAO 2017).

Demands for Quality from the Rising Middle-Class Consumer

Urban populations, growing at a steady pace, are diverse and partly composed of an emerging middle class. A report by Deloitte Touche Tohmatsu cited by Lançon and Boyer (2019, 34) estimates that in 2013 the middle class[7] in Africa represented 34 percent of the population, or 355 million people.[8] The Deloitte study notes that in Africa in the three decades preceding 2010, "the emerging middle class experienced a growth rate of 3.1 percent, compared to 2.6 percent for the total population." Higher-income middle-class consumers view food quality as increasingly important, seeking freshness, flavor, and specific origins. They are altering their purchasing habits in order to avoid health issues caused by excessive exposure to pesticides (Lançon and Boyer 2019), particularly in middle-income North African and Asian countries, where the middle classes are more numerous and farmers are more reliant on chemical inputs.

Aderghal, Lemeilleur, and Romagny (2019, 6) note that in Morocco "changes in urban demand are not linear. Beyond increasingly important quantitative issues, consumer demand is evolving qualitatively with the development of various urban social classes and very differentiated practices." The emergence of middle-class consumers (Ncube 2011) has resulted in more varied diets, with more fruits, vegetables and fresh products, and shorter food preparation time. In Côte d'Ivoire and Niger, supermarkets reflect this dynamic to a lesser extent. D'Angelo and Brisson (2019, 109) find that in Niamey "the recent emergence of modern supermarkets [is meeting] middle-class [consumer] demands of middle-class consumers for [good] quality, hygiene, and variety." Citing Poyau (2005), Lançon and Boyer (2019, 19) found that "supermarket-style commercial infrastructure … is emerging in the 'affluent/wealthy' neighborhoods of the economic capital [Abidjan] of Côte d'Ivoire. [This] type of infrastructure is, therefore, intended for the 'richest' populations."

Cities: Not as Poor as Rural Areas on Average, but Seeing Increasing Poverty and Rural–Urban Migration
The numerous urban poor have their own food-related problems because food takes a big bite out of their small household budgets. The price elasticity of food is high, with price affecting consumption decisions. In the broadest sense of the term, food expenditures include purchase price and transport costs. Compared with middle-class consumers, the poor care less about quality when making food purchase decisions. According to Bricas (2017), the poor cannot afford to buy sufficiently nutritious and safe food products, and they are also very vulnerable to price increases. World Bank (2020b) data confirm that this is particularly true in Côte d'Ivoire, where 36 percent of city dwellers lived below the poverty line in 2015. Niger also has a large percentage of urban poor, with 19 percent living below the poverty line. Morocco, by contrast, has recently seen a decline in urban poverty, from nearly 10 percent in the late 1990s to less than 5 percent in 2007, the latest available census year.

Overall, food represents a large part of household spending. On average, food consumes 44 percent of household budgets in Sub-Saharan Africa, reaching 54 percent in Côte d'Ivoire and a surprisingly high 44 percent in Morocco (graph 1.3). The Engel curve, which depicts the lessening relationship between household income and food's share of household spending, also shows that food's share of spending is much higher in low-income households (Lozano-Garcia and Young 2014). For example, in Niger the food expenditure falls from 60 percent for the first quintile to less than 50 percent for the fifth. In Côte d'Ivoire, this gradient declines from 50 percent to 30 percent.

Graph 1.3 **Food as a Share of Household Spending**

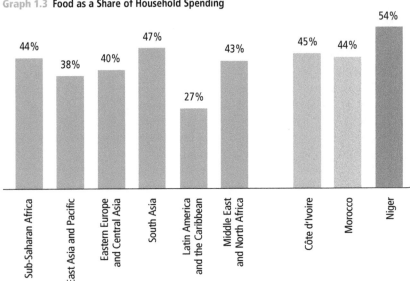

Source: World Bank, Global Consumption Database, 2010, http://datatopics.worldbank.org/consumption/.

The Contribution of Lower Transport Costs to Trade Globalization

Formal Imports: Increasing and Diversifying the Food Supply

Urban poverty increases consumer demand for low-cost products, which often favors imports. For example, D'Angelo and Brisson (2019, 38) found that in Niger, "locally produced fish was sold for about XOF [CFAF] 1,250 per kilo versus XOF 800–1,000 for imported frozen fish."[9] Similarly, according to Lançon and Boyer (2019), Côte d'Ivoire imports massive amounts of rice (803,000 tons in 2013), mainly from India and Thailand because domestic rice is often more expensive than its Asian competitors. Local production must battle highly subsidized competition from many foreign countries (*Sciences et Avenir* 2015). At the macroeconomic level, the general rise in import volumes into Africa reflects demand for lower-priced products, as reported by Bricas, Tchamda, and Mouton (2016).

Graph 1.4 shows a clear upward trend in the quantity of West African and North African grain imports since 1961 (illustrated relative to population size to account for population growth). If the analysis is limited to Côte d'Ivoire, Morocco, and Niger the pronounced increase in imports between 1995 and 2016 is more pronounced. The value of imported foods, excluding fish imports, rose by three times in Côte d'Ivoire, two and a half times in Morocco, and five times in Niger.

To verify that the increase in grain imports was not solely due to population growth, graph 1.5 shows the evolution of imports per capita in the three countries studied. The upward momentum observed at the regional level is found in each of the three countries, confirming the idea that food imports to Côte d'Ivoire, Morocco, and Niger are fairly representative of the region.

Graph 1.4 **Grain Imports: West Africa and North Africa, 1960–2013**

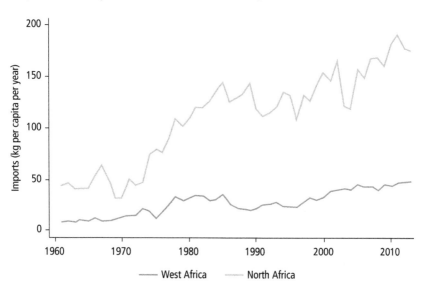

Source: Food and Agriculture Organization Corporate Statistical Database (FAOSTAT), 2020, http://www.fao.org/faostat/fr/#data/TP.

Graph 1.5 **Grain Imports: Côte d'Ivoire, Morocco, and Niger, 1960–2013**

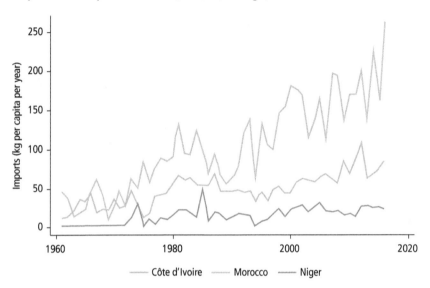

Source: Food and Agriculture Organization Corporate Statistical Database (FAOSTAT), 2020, http://www.fao.org/faostat/fr/#data/TP.

In Africa in general, new imports are mainly destined for cities. This is consistent with the emergence of a poor urban population that can hardly resort to feeding itself because urban areas have little to no place for subsistence farming.

Graph 1.6, based on Bricas, Tchamba, and Mouton (2016) and data gathered in 2001 and 2007 on Cameroonian households by the Enquête camerounaise auprès des ménages (ECAM), shows the origin of products according to where they were consumed in Cameroon. The increase in imported products affects each of the product consumption areas, especially the larger cities. Between 2001 and 2007, the share of imported food to be locally processed or ready to eat increased by more than 5 percentage points in principal cities and remained almost constant in secondary cities. The share of imported food was almost negligible in rural areas, where imports do not seem to be on a strong uptrend (Republic of Cameroon 2002, 2008).

Graph 1.6 Origin of Food Products Consumed in Cameroon by Rural and Urban Area, 2001 and 2007

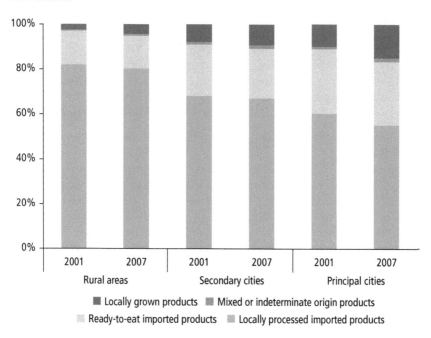

Source: Bricas, Tchamba, and Mouton 2016; Republic of Cameroon 2002, 2008.

Diversifying the Food Supply, Especially According to Season

Imports also play a role in nutrition by constituting an increasing share of the available food in Africa. Bricas, Tchamda, and Mouton (2016) have described the increase in food availability observed there. It appears that the increase in imports mainly provides the newly available calories. In particular, imported grains and vegetable oils contribute significantly to increasing food availability[10] in the region. In Côte d'Ivoire, Morocco, and Niger, the nutritional role of imports also appears confirmed. The food dependency ratio indicates the share of imports in local consumption, reporting on the level of imports to local production, net of the trade balance. For example, between 2005 and 2016 the grains food dependency ratio[11] increased from 51.7 percent to 53.5 percent in Côte d'Ivoire (FAOSTAT 2017a) and rose from 39.1 percent to 42.1 percent in Morocco (FAOSTAT 2017b).

Imports thus make it possible to diversify the food supply. More counter-cyclical, they increase during seasons when local production is at its lowest. In Niger, for example, tomato imports are very cyclical, and volumes change over the course of the year (D'Angelo and Brisson 2019). During the local low production period, imported tomatoes from Burkina Faso supplement the local Nigerian supply because at that point prices are high in Niger and the two countries have similar growing seasons. Conversely, Burkina Faso's tomatoes do not appear in Nigerian markets from late February to mid-March, when prices are lowest and local production is abundant. During Niger's rainy season from June to August, local tomatoes are absent from the market. The price of tomatoes thus increases at the same time that the imports arrive, often from Ghana and Benin, where the growing seasons differ from that of Niger.

The Role of Imports in Stabilizing Prices When Domestic Production Collapses

Imports also help overcome a lack of local production during crises. The 2008 global food crisis prompted food riots in many African countries, particularly Côte d'Ivoire and Niger. Both countries responded by suspending import taxes on food products (FAO, no date), resulting in a significant increase in imports. Lançon and Boyer (2019) note that following the food crisis in 2009, Côte d'Ivoire spent CFAF 235 billion (€380 million) to import a massive 919,000 tons of white rice, whereas in 2013 it imported only 803,000 tons.

However, these measures benefit an entire country only when its markets are integrated. In fact, isolated and rural areas do not receive imported products. Governments have set up price and redistribution monitoring systems to integrate markets and curb the effect of shortages. Often, such systems are based on using imports. For example, in Niger the Office des Produits Vivriers du Niger (OPVN, or Niger Food Products Office) obtains its supplies from wholesalers that import foods and store stocks of food around the country. These stocks are then passed to towns and villages, which in turn distribute the food through a sales committee. Food allocation decisions draw on market information systems that monitor certain basic food product prices in various markets. When the system registers a sharp rise in prices, it activates the OPVN redistribution system (D'Angelo and Brisson 2019). According to Bricas (2017), the dependency on imported food must be put in perspective. He notes that most imports are starchy commodities, which account for only about one-third of the food consumed. Local or regional producers supply the other two-thirds. Roughly equal parts animal and other products, they provide a smaller share of the calories consumed, but their nutritional role is crucial.

Conclusion

Côte d'Ivoire, Morocco, and Niger are experiencing overall population growth, rising urban populations, and international trade integration. These forces tend to affect local food demand in terms of both volume and composition. The emergence of middle-class consumers who value food quality has contributed to the emergence of supermarkets, which have reorganized traditional food supply networks in order to meet quality standards and ensure a constant supply. At the base of the socioeconomic pyramid, the urban poor have a very elastic food demand predicated on price because of their very constrained budgets.

Moreover, the three countries have also integrated local production and consumption into international food value chains. By doing so, they meet the requirements of urban consumers by ensuring a continual supply of certain foods—regardless of season—and by supplying some cheaper products. Much like supermarkets, food imports affect local production by increasing consumer demand for quality. Food-importing countries and companies, and even local consumers, impose quality standards on all products traded. Requirements for high quality tend to affect local farms by giving large agricultural enterprises an advantage. However, some arrangements allow small farmers to respond to the new requirements, especially when smallholders benefit from assistance programs or cooperate with one another to ensure constant and abundant supplies of products.

Chapter 2 now turns to an examination of the physical market infrastructure, describing how it affects and locates food supply and distribution circuits. The authors discuss ways in which urban densification and imports availability often change urban and suburban farms, pushing them farther away from the city. It also looks at the question of optimal locations for urban wholesale and retail markets and the forces that determine a market's success or failure. In addition to discussing physical facilities, including storage, cold chain–compliant facilities, and the state of roads and other transport infrastructure, chapter 2 highlights the importance of so-called spatial frictions in the sense of geographical economics—that is, a concept based on the notion that distance usually requires some amount of effort, energy, time, or other resources (or some combination of these) to overcome. In the case of markets, supply centralization, which reduces spatial frictions, allows some intermediaries to exercise monopoly power over certain sectors.

Chapter 2 concludes with an in-depth analysis of governance structures for each of the three case studies in order to understand how public authorities and donors can work together in these complex contexts. Chapter 3 focuses on the parameters that determine many trade relationships. Because food supply and distribution not only concern physical infrastructure and price, but also require information dissemination, credit access, and merchant networks, chapter 3 looks at the institutions that condition market operations, identifies some institutional dysfunctions, and gives reasons for some of the inefficiencies.

Notes

1. Many expressions are used synonymously. Alongside the term *food system* as defined in the text, there is also the term *food value chain*. Both terms generally refer to all production activities through distribution, including financing. The term *food value chain* emerged in mid-1990s studies that focused on globalization and its impact on the value added by various activities and actors during the food production and distribution. *Food value chain* is very close to the French term *agricultural sector* (*secteur agricole*), in use since the 1960s. The term *food supply and distribution systems* or *food supply and distribution chain*, or simply food chain, is also widely used to describe all food production and distribution activities, but with less inclusion of remuneration and regulation than the other terms.
2. Unless otherwise indicated, the statistics in this paragraph are from Allen, Heinrigs, and Heo (2018).
3. For more information, see the Milan Urban Food Policy Pact site: https://www.milan urbanfoodpolicypact.org/.
4. This section relies on Lemeilleur, Aderghal, et al. (2019).
5. "Informal" can be simply defined as escaping state registration and regulation. However, many informal actors actually contribute to public resources by, for example, paying market taxes.
6. The Morocco case study covers the conurbation of Rabat, Salé, and Témara. For the sake of brevity, this volume refers to the overall urban area as Rabat.
7. People with per capita expenditures of from $2 to $20 a day are considered part of the African middle class. However, the definition of lower- and upper-middle classes distinguishes between individuals with per capita expenditures of between $4 and $10 and between $10 and $20 per day, respectively (Lançon and Boyer 2019).
8. According to Lançon and Boyer (2019), "Individuals with per capita consumption levels of $2.00 to $4.00 a day belong to the so-called 'floating' population [of the middle class]. A slight change in the cost of living can indeed push them back into poverty, which makes them extremely vulnerable. As a result, the figure of 355 million middle-class Africans may have been overestimated."
9. D'Angelo and Brisson (2019) explain that frozen food imports to Niger often come from China and Thailand via Benin.
10. Food availability is based on national production and trade statistics: production + imports – exports – nonfood uses (such as seeds, animal feed, and industrial uses) – field and storage losses + inventory change between the beginning and end of the year (Bricas, Tchamda, and Mouton 2016).
11. Ratio of grain imports to the sum of local production and the opposite of the grain trade balance.

References

Aderghal, M., S. Lemeilleur, and B. Romagny. 2019. "Contribution des systèmes de distribution alimentaire à la sécurité alimentaire des villes: étude de cas sur l'agglomé-ration de Rabat (Maroc)" [The contribution of food distribution systems to urban food security: Case study of Rabat, Morocco]. Notes techniques, No. 48, Agence française de développement, Paris, February. https://www.afd.fr/fr/nt-48-systeme-alimentaire -qualite-sanitaire-aderghal-lemeilleur-romagny.

AFD (Agence française de développement). 2015. "L'AFD et les équipements marchands urbains: 30 ans de projets de réhabilitation de marchés en Afrique" [AFD and urban commercial facilities: 30 years of market rehabilitation projects in Africa]. AFD, Paris, September. https://www.afd.fr/fr/evaluationde-trois-projets-de-rehabilitation-de -marches-centraux-mahajanga-ouagadougouet-phnom-penh.

AFD (Agence française de développement). 2017. "L'AFD et l'alimentation des villes, quel rôle pour les collectivités locales?" [AFD and urban food: What role can local governments play?]. AFD, Paris, September. https://www.afd.fr/fr/lafd-et-l -alimentation-des-villes.

Aguié, A. G. 1997. "Le marché de gros de Bouaké: une expérience pour l'Afrique" [The Bouaké wholesale market: An experiment for Africa]. Aliments pour les villes, AC/06-97F, FAO/AGSM/SADA, Rome.

Ahmed, A. U., R. V. Hill, L. C. Smith, D. M. Wiesmann, and T. Frankenberger. 2007. "The World's Most Deprived: Characteristics and Causes of Extreme Poverty and Hunger." 2020 Discussion Paper 43, International Food Policy Research Institute, Washington, DC, October.

Aker, J. C. 2008. "Does Digital Divide or Provide? The Impact of Cell Phones on Grain Markets in Niger." BREAD Working Paper 177, Bureau for Research and Economic Analysis of Development (BREAD), London School of Economics. http://www.oecd .org/countries/niger/41713177.pdf.

Aker, J. C., and I. M. Mbiti 2010. "Mobile Phones and Economic Development in Africa." *Journal of Economic Perspectives* 24 (3): 207–32.

Allen, T. 2017. "Le coût des prix alimentaires élevés en Afrique de l'Ouest" [The cost of high food prices in West Africa]. Notes ouest-africaines, No. 8, Organisation for Economic Co-operation and Development, Paris.

Allen, T., and P. Heinrigs. 2016. "Les nouvelles opportunités de l'économie alimentaire ouest-africaine" [New opportunities for the West African food economy]. Notes ouest-africaines, No. 1, Organisation for Economic Co-operation and Development, Paris.

Allen, T., P. Heinrigs, and I. Heo. 2018. "Agriculture, alimentation et emploi en Afrique de l'Ouest" [Agriculture, food, and employment in West Africa]. Notes ouest-africaines, No. 14, Organisation for Economic Co-operation and Deveopment, Paris.

Balineau, G., and N. Madariaga. 2019. "Repenser l'alimentation dans les villes du Sud" [Rethinking food in the urban South]. Question de développement, No. 45, Agence française de développement, Paris, September.

Balineau, G., N. Madariaga, A. Françoise, and J.-R. Cuzon. Forthcoming. "Villes et systèmes agro-alimentaires durables: repenser le rôle des marchés—principes d'inter-vention pour des projets renouvelés" [Cities and sustainable food systems: Rethinking the role of markets—intervention principles for updated projects]. Rapport technique, Agence française de développement, Paris.

Bignebat, C., A. A. Koç, and S. Lemeilleur. 2009. "Small Producers, Supermarkets, and the Role of Intermediaries in Turkey's Fresh Fruit and Vegetable Market." *Agricultural Economics* 40: 807–16.

Bricas, N. 2017. "Les enjeux de l'urbanisation pour la durabilité des systèmes alimentaires" [Urbanization's challenges to food system sustainability]. In *Construire des politiques alimentaires urbaines* [Designing urban food policies], edited by C. Brand, N. Bricas, D. Conaré, B. Daviron, J. Debru, L. Michel, and T. Soulard, 19–42. Versailles: Éditions Quae.

Bricas, N., C. Tchamda, and F. Mouton, eds. 2016. "L'Afrique à la conquête de son marché alimentaire intérieur: enseignements de dix ans d'enquêtes auprès des ménages d'Afrique de l'Ouest, du Cameroun et du Tchad" [Africa tries to conquer its domestic food market: Lessons from 10 years of household surveys in West Africa, Cameroon, and Chad]. Études de l'AFD, No. 12, 132, Agence française de développement, Paris. https://www.afd.fr/fr/lafrique-la-conquete-de-son-marche-alimentaire-interieur-enseignements-de-dix-ans-denquetes-aupres-des-menages-dafrique-de-louest-du-cameroun-et-du-tchad.

Broutin, C., and N. Bricas. 2006. Agroalimentaire et lutte contre la pauvreté en *Afrique subsaharienne: le rôle des micro et petites entreprises* [Food and the fight against poverty in Sub-Saharan Africa: The role of micro and small enterprises]. Paris: Éditions du Gret.

Byerlee, D., A. F. Garcia, A. Giertz, and V. Palmade. 2013. "Growing Africa: Unlocking the Potential of Agribusiness." World Bank, Washington, DC. http://documents.worldbank.org/curated/en/327811467990084951/pdf/756630v10REPLA0frica0pub03011013web.pdf.

Caldeira, E., and G. Rota-Graziosi. 2014. "La décentralisation dans les pays en développement: une revue de la littérature" [Decentralization in developing countries: A review of the literature]. Études et documents, No. 11, CERDI, Paris.

Caldeira, E., G. Rota-Graziosi, and M. Foucault. 2012. "Does Decentralization Facilitate Access to Poverty-Related Services? Evidence from Benin." NBER Working Paper No. 18118, National Bureau of Economic Research (NBER), Cambridge, MA.

Calmette, F. Forthcoming. "Le rôle des marchés dans l'approvisionnement alimentaire des villes: un agenda de recherche basé sur la théorie" [The role of markets in urban food supply: A research agenda based on theory]. Papiers de recherche, Agence française de développement, Paris.

Calmette, F., and P. Bontems. Forthcoming. "Infrastructures et territoires" [Infrastructures and territories]. Papiers de recherche, Agence française de développement, Paris.

Chaléard, J.-L. 1996. *Temps des villes, temps des vivres: l'essor du vivrier marchand en Côte d'Ivoire* [City times, food times: The rise of cash crops in Côte d'Ivoire]. Paris: Karthala.

Chaléard, J.-L. 1998. "Croissance urbaine et production vivrière" [Urban growth and food production] *Afrique contemporaine* (185): 3–17.

Choi, J., M. Dutz, and Z. Usman. 2019. "The Future of Work in Africa: Harnessing the Potential of Digital Technologies for All." World Bank, Washington, DC. https://openknowledge.worldbank.org/handle/10986/32124 License: CC BY 3.0 IGO.

Cour, J.-M. 2004. "Peuplement, urbanisation et transformation de l'agriculture: un cadre d'analyse démo-économique et spatial" [Settlement, urbanization and agricultural transformation: A demographic, economic and spatial analytical framework]. Cahiers agricultures 13 (1): 158–65.

D'Angelo, L., and E. Brisson. 2019. "Systèmes d'approvisionnement et de distribution alimentaires: étude de cas sur la ville de Niamey (Niger)" [Food supply and distribution systems: Case study on the city of Niamey, Niger]. Notes techniques, No. 50, Agence française de développement, Paris, February. https://www.afd.fr/fr/nt-50 -marche-alimentation-distribution-groupe8-brisson-emile-geay-dangelo.

Desmet, K., and E. Rossi-Hansberg. 2014. "Spatial Development." *American Economic Review* 104 (4): 1211–43.

Ekanem, E. O. 1998. "The Street Food Trade in Africa: Safety and Socio-Environmental Issues." *Food Control* 9 (4): 211–15.

Fafchamps, M., and R. V. Hill. 2005. "Selling at the Farm-Gate or Travelling to Market?" *American Journal of Agricultural Economics* 87 (3): 717–34.

FAO (Food and Agriculture Organization of the United Nations). 2013. *Food Wastage Footprint: Impacts on Natural Resources, Summary Report.* Rome: FAO.

FAO (Food and Agriculture Organization of the United Nations). 2014. *Food Wastage Footprint: Full Cost Accounting, Final Report.* Rome: FAO.

FAO (Food and Agriculture Organization of the United Nations). 2017. *The State of Food and Agriculture: Leveraging Food Systems for Inclusive Rural Transformation.* Rome: FAO. http://www.fao.org/3/a-I7658e.pdf.

FAO (Food and Agriculture Organization of the United Nations). 2018. *Sustainable Food Systems: Concept and Framework.* Rome: FAO. http://www.fao.org/3/ca2079en/CA 2079EN.pdf.

FAO (Food and Agriculture Organization of the United Nations). 2020. "SAVE FOOD: Global Initiative on Food Loss and Waste Reduction." Rome.

FAO (Food and Agriculture Organization of the United Nations). No date. "Effectiveness of Policy Responses to the 2008 Food Crisis: Evidence from Five Countries in West Africa." Policy Brief, FAO Regional Office for Africa. http://www.fao.org/3/an172e /an172e00.pdf.

FAO (Food and Agriculture Organization of the United Nations), WHO (World Health Organization), IFAD (International Fund for Agricultural Development), WFP (World Food Programme), and UNICEF (United Nations Children's Fund). 2018. "The State of Food Security and Nutrition in the World 2018: Building Climate Resilience for Food Security and Nutrition." FAO, Rome.

FAOSTAT (Food and Agriculture Organization Corporate Statistical Database). 2017. "Morocco Static Statistics." FAO Statistics Division, Rome. http://faostat.fao.org/static /syb/syb_143.pdf.

Farina, E. 2002. "Consolidation, Multinationalisation, and Competition in Brazil: Impacts on Horticulture and Dairy Product Systems." *Development Policy Review* 20 (4): 441–57.

Galannakis, C. 2018. "Food Waste Recovery: Prospects and Opportunities." In *Sustainable Food Systems from Agriculture to Industry: Improving Production and Processing*, edited by C. Campanhola and S. Pandey. Amsterdam: Elsevier Science and Technology Books.

Galtier, F., and J. Egg. 2003. "Le 'paradoxe' des systèmes d'information de marché (SIM): une clef de lecture issue de l'économie institutionnelle et de la théorie de la communication" [The paradox of market information systems (MIS): A lens drawn from institutional economics and communication theory]. *Économies et Sociétés* (41): 1227–60.

Gollin, D., R. Jedwab, and D. Vollrath. 2016. "Urbanization with and without Industrialization." *Journal of Economic Growth* 21 (1): 35–70.

Goosens, F., B. Minten, and E. Tollens. 1994. *Nourrir Kinshasa. L'approvisionnement local d'une métropole africaine* [Feeding Kinshasa: Local supply to an African metropolis]. Paris: L'Harmattan.

Groupe Huit. 2015. "Diagnostic de l'armature commerciale de la ville de Niamey" [An analysis of the City of Niamey's commercial armature]. Final report, Groupe Huit, Montrouge, France. https://reca-.niger.org/IMG/pdf/AFD_Groupe_Huit_Rapport _armature_commerciale_Niamey_final_re_duit.pdf.

Guyer, J. 1987. *Feeding African Cities: Studies in Regional Social History*. Manchester, U.K.: Manchester University Press.

Harris-White, B. 1996. *A Political Economy of Agricultural Markets in South Asia*. London: Sage Publications.

Henson, S. 2003. "The Economics of Food Safety in Developing Countries." ESA Working Paper, Vol. 19, No. 3, 19–30, Agricultural Development Economics Division, Food and Agriculture Organization of the United Nations, New York.

Hugon, P. 1985. "Le miroir sans tain. Dépendance alimentaire et urbanisation en Afrique: un essai d'analyse en termes de filières" [The one-way mirror. Food dependence and urbanization in Africa: An analysis of value chains]. In *Nourrir les villes* [Feeding cities], edited by Altersial, Ceredm and M.S.A., 9–46. Paris: L'Harmattan.

IFAD (International Fund for Agricultural Development). 2017. "Policy Brief—Promoting Integrated and Inclusive Rural-Urban Dynamics and Food Systems."Rome, June. https://www.ifad.org/en/web/knowledge/publication/asset/40256615.

IFPRI (International Food Policy Research Institute). 2017. *Global Food Report 2017*. Washington, DC: IFPRI. https://www.ifpri.org/cdmref/p15738coll2/id/131085 /filename/131296.pdf.

Jensen, R. 2007. "The Digital Provide: Information (Technology), Market Performance, and Welfare in the South Indian Fisheries Sector." *Quarterly Journal of Economics* 122 (3): 879–924.

Jones, W. O. 1972. *Marketing Staple Food Crops in Tropical Africa*. Ithaca, NY: Cornell University Press.

Lall, S. V., J. V. Henderson, and A. J. Venables. 2017. *Africa's Cities: Opening Doors to the World*. Washington, DC: World Bank.

Lançon, F., and A. Boyer. 2019. "Contribution des systèmes de distribution alimentaire à la sécurité alimentaire des villes: étude de cas sur l'agglomération d'Abidjan (Côte d'Ivoire)" [The contribution of food distribution systems to urban food security: Case study of Abidjan, Côte d'Ivoire]. Notes techniques, No. 49, Agence française de développement, Paris, February. https://www.afd.fr/fr/nt-49-systeme-alimentaire -urbanisation-abidjan-lancon-boyer.

Lemeilleur, S., M. Aderghal, O. Jenani, A. Binane, M. Berja, Y. Medaoui, and P. Moustier. 2019. "La distance est-elle toujours importante pour organiser l'approvisionnement alimentaire urbain? Le cas de l'agglomération de Rabat" [Is distance always important for urban food supply production? The case of Greater Rabat]. Papiers de recherche, No. 91, Agence française de développement, Paris. https://www.afd.fr/fr/la-distance -est-elle-toujours-importante-pour-organiser-lapprovisionnement-alimentaire-urbain -le-cas-de-lagglomeration-de-rabat.

Lemeilleur, S., L. D'Angelo, M. Rousseau, E. Brisson, A. Boyet, F. Lançon, and P. Moustier. 2019. "Les systèmes de distribution alimentaire dans les pays d'Afrique méditerranéenne et subsaharienne: repenser le rôle des marchés dans l'infrastructure commerciale" [Food distribution systems in Mediterranean and Sub-Saharan African countries: Rethinking the market's role in trade infrastructure]. Notes techniques, No. 51, Agence française de développement, Paris, February. https://www.afd.fr/fr/nt-51-marche-alimentation-distribution-lemeilleur-dangelo-rousseau-brisson-boyet-lancon-moustier.

Lipton, M. 1977. *Why Poor People Stay Poor: A Study of Urban Bias in Economic Development*. London: Temple Smith.

Lozano-Gracia, N., and C. Young. 2014. *Housing Consumption and Urbanization*. Washington, DC: World Bank.

Maire, B., and F. Delpeuch. 2004. "La transition nutritionnelle, l'alimentation et les villes dans les pays en développement" [The nutritional transition, food, and cities in developing countries]. *Cahiers Agricultures* 13 (1): 23–30.

Michelon, B. 2008. "La gouvernance dans les projets d'équipements marchands en Afrique." Paper prepared for 12th EADI General Conference, Global Governance for Sustainable Development, École Polytechnique Fédérale de Lausanne, Geneva.

Moustier, P. 2017. "Short Urban Food Chains in Developing Countries: Signs of the Past or of the Future?" *Natures Sciences Sociétés* 25 (1): 7–20.

Moustier, P., M. Figuié, D. Te Anh, and T. T. L. Nguyen. 2009. "Are Supermarkets Poorfriendly? Debates and Evidence from Vietnam." In *Controversies in Food and Agricultural Marketing*, edited by A. Lindgreen and M. Hinghley, 311–25. Aldershot, U.K.: Gower Publishing Ltd.

Nakamura, S., R. Harati, S. Lall, Y. Dikhanov, N. Hamadeh, W. V. Oliver, M. O. Rissanen, and M. Yamanaka. 2016. "Is Living in African Cities Expensive?" Policy Research Working Paper 7641, World Bank, Washington, DC.

Ncube, M. 2011. *Africa in 50 Years' Time: The Road towards Inclusive Growth*. Tunis: African Development Bank.

Paloviita, A., and M. Jarvela. 2015. *Climate Change Adaptation and Food Supply Chain Management*. London and New York: Routledge.

Poyau, A. 2005. "Les récentes mutations des marchés urbains dans la capitale économique ivoirienne" [Recent changes in urban markets in the Ivorian economic capital]. *Espace, Populations Sociétés* (1): 111–126.

Quattri, M. 2012. "On Trade Efficiency in the Ethiopian Agricultural Markets." Paper prepared for 123rd EAAE Seminar, Dublin, February 23–24.

Raton, G. 2012."Les foires au Mali, de l'approvisionnement urbain à l'organisation de l'espace rural: le cas de la périphérie de Bamako" [Fairs in Mali, from urban supply to the organization of rural space: The case of the outskirts of Bamako]. PhD diss., University Panthéon-Sorbonne-Paris I School of Geography.

Ravallion, M., S. Chen, and P. Sangraula. 2007. "New Evidence on the Urbanization of Global Poverty." *Population and Development Review* 33 (4): 667–701.

Reardon, T. 2012. *The Global Rise and Impact of Supermarkets: An International Perspective*. Proceedings of Crawford Fund 17th Annual Parliamentary Conference, The Supermarket Revolution in Food: Good, Bad or Ugly for the World's Farmers, Consumers and Retailers? August 14–16, 2011, Crawford Fund, Canberra, Australia.

Reardon, T., C. B. Barrett, J. A. Berdegué, and J. F. M. Swinnen. 2009. "Agrifood Industry Transformation and Small Farmers in Developing Countries." *World Development* 37 (11): 1717–27.

Reardon, T., D. Bereuter, and D. Glickman. 2016. *Growing Food for Growing Cities: Transforming Food Systems in an Urbanizing World.* Chicago: Chicago Council on Global Affairs.

Reardon, T., C. P. Timmer, C. B. Barrett, and J. Berdegué. 2003. "The Rise of Supermarkets in Africa, Asia, and Latin America." *American Journal of Agricultural Economics* 85 (5): 1140–46.

Reardon, T., C. P. Timmer, and B. Minten. 2012. "Supermarket Revolution in Asia and Emerging Development Strategies to Include Small Farmers." *Proceedings of the National Academy of Sciences* 109 (31): 12332–37.

Republic of Cameroon. 2002. "Deuxième Enquête Camerounaise Auprès des Ménages: pauvreté, habitat et cadre de vie au Cameroun en 2001 [Second Cameroonian Household Survey: Poverty, housing, and lifestyle in Cameroon in 2001]. National Institute of Statistics, Yaoundé. http://www.minhdu.gov.cm/documents/ecampauvretehabitat.pdf.

Republic of Cameroon. 2008. "Troisième Enquête Camerounaise Auprès des Ménages: tendances, profil et déterminants de la pauvreté au Cameroun entre 2001–2007 [Third Cameroonian Household Survey: Poverty trends, profile, and determinants in Cameroon from 2001 to 2007]. National Institute of Statistics, Yaoundé. https://catalog.ihsn.org/index.php/catalog/2256/related-materials.

Requier-Desjardins, D. 1991. "La ville comme facteur de développement: le cas de l'Afrique subsaharienne" [The city as a development factor: The case of Sub-Saharan Africa]. *Problèmes économiques* 233 (2): 15–20.

Riley, H. M., and J. M. Staatz. 1993. "Food System Organization Problems in Developing Countries." In *Agricultural and Food Marketing in Developing Countries: Selected Readings*, edited by J. Abbott. Wallingford, U.K.: CAB International.

Rousseau, M., A. Boyet, and T. Harroud. 2019. "Le makhzen et le marché de gros: la politique d'approvisionnement des villes marocaines entre contrôle social et néo-libéralisme" [The governing elite and the wholesale market: The supply policy of Moroccan cities straddles social control and neoliberalism]. Papiers de recherche, No. 92, Agence française de développement, Paris. https://www.afd.fr/fr/le-makhzen-et-le-marche-de-gros-la-politique-dapprovisionnement-des-villes-marocaines-entre-controle-social-et-neoliberalisme.

Rousseau, M., and T. Harroud. 2019. "Mutation de la gouvernance des systèmes alimentaires urbains: le cas de l'agglomération de Rabat-Salé" [Changes in urban food system governance: The case of Rabat-Salé]. Notes techniques, No. 47, Agence française de développement, Paris, February. https://www.afd.fr/fr/nt-47-systeme-alimentaire-rabat-rousseau-harroud.

Satterthwaite, D., G. McGranahan, and C. Tacoli. 2010. "Urbanization and Its Implications for Food and Farming." *Philosophical Transactions of the Royal Society B: Biological Sciences* 365 (1554): 2809–20.

Sciences et Avenir. 2015. "La Côte d'Ivoire en quête d'autosuffisance en riz" [Côte d'Ivoire seeks rice self-sufficiency]. *Sciences et Avenir*, August 11. https://www.sciencesetavenir.fr/nature-environnement/agriculture-la-cote-d-ivoire-en-quete-d-autosuffisance-en-riz_101277.

Staatz, J. M., J. Dione, and N. N. Dembele. 1989. "Cereals Market Liberalization in Mali." *World Development* 17 (5): 703–18.

Straub, S. 2019. "Transport Infrastructure and the Spatial Evolution of the Productive Structure in Brazil." Research paper, No. 107, Agence française de développement, Paris.

Tefft, J. F., M. Jonasova, R. T. O. A. Adjao, and A. M. Morgan. 2017. *Food Systems for an Urbanizing World: Knowledge Product.* Washington, DC: World Bank and Food and Agriculture Organization of the United Nations. http://documents.worldbank.org/curated/en/454961511210702794/Food-systems-for-an-urbanizing-world-knowledge-product.

Timmer, C. P., W. P. Falcon, and S. R. Pearson. 1983. *Food Policy Analysis.* Baltimore: Johns Hopkins University Press.

Tollens, E. 1997. "Wholesale Markets in African Cities: Diagnosis, Role, Advantages and Elements for Further Study and Development." Food Supply and Distribution to Cities in French-Speaking Africa—Food into Cities Collection, AC/05-97, Food and Agriculture Organization of the United Nations and University de Louvain, Rome. http://www.fao.org/3/a-ab790e.pdf.

Tschirley, D., M. Ayieko, M. Hichaambwa, J. Goeb, and W. Loescher. 2010. "Modernizing Africa's Fresh Produce Supply Chains without Rapid Supermarket Takeover: Towards a Definition of Research and Investment Priorities." MSU International Development Working Paper, No. 106, Michigan State University, East Lansing.

UNCTAD (United Nations Conference on Trade and Development). 2017. "Trade and Development Report 2017: Beyond Austerity: Towards a Global New Deal."UNCTAD, Geneva. https://unctad.org/en/PublicationsLibrary/tdr2017_en.pdf.

United Nations. 2015. *World Urbanization Prospects: The 2014 Revision.* ST/ESA/SER. A/366, UN Department of Economic and Social Affairs, Population Division, New York. https://population.un.org/wup/Publications/Files/WUP2014-Report.pdf.

United Nations. 2017. "New Urban Agenda." United Nations Habitat III Secretariat, New York. http://habitat3.org/wp-content/uploads/NUA-English.pdf.

Van Wesenbeeck, C. F. A. 2018. "Disentangling Urban and Rural Food Security in West Africa." West African Papers 15, Organisation for Economic Co-operation and Development, Paris.

Vennetier, P. 1972a."L'approvisionnement des villes en Afrique noire: un problème à étudier" [Urba n supply in black Africa: A problem to study]. In *Études de géographie tropicales offertes à P. Gourou* [Tropical geography studies for P. Gourou], 477–90. Paris: Mouton.

Vennetier, P., ed. 1972b. "Dix études sur l'approvisionnement des villes" [Ten studies of urban supply]. Travaux et documents de géographie tropicale, No. 7, CEGET-CNRS, Bordeaux.

Vermeulen, S. J., B. M. Campbell, and J. S. Ingram. 2012. "Climate Change and Food Systems." *Annual Review of Environment and Resources* (37): 195–222.

Von Thünen, J. H. 1826. *Der isolierte Staat in Beziehung auf Landwirtschaft und Natio-nalökonomie.* Hamburg: Perthes. Translation: *The Isolated State,* 1966. Oxford, U.K.: Pergamon Press.

Vorley, B. 2013. *Meeting Small-Scale Farmers in Their Markets: Understanding and Improving the Institutions and Governance of Informal Agri-food Trace.* London: International Institute for Environment and Development.

Weatherspoon, D., J. Oehmke, A. Dembele, M. Coleman, T. Satimanon, and L. Weatherspoon. 2013. "Price and Expenditure Elasticities for Fresh Fruits in an Urban Food Desert." *Urban Studies* 50 (1): 88–106.

Weatherspoon, D., J. Oehmke, A. Dembele, and L. Weatherspoon. 2015. "Fresh Vegetable Demand Behaviour in an Urban Food Desert." *Urban Studies* 52 (5): 960–79.

Weatherspoon, D. D., and T. Reardon. 2003."The Rise of Supermarkets in Africa: Implications for Agrifood Systems and the Rural Poor." *Development Policy Review* (21): 333–55.

Winarno, F. G., and A. Allain. 1991. "Street Foods in Developing Countries: Lessons from Asia." *Food, Nutrition and Agriculture* (11): 11–18.

Woldu, T., G. Abebe, I. Lamoot, and B. Minten. 2013. "Urban Food Retail in Africa: The Case of Addis Ababa, Ethiopia." ESSP Working Paper, No. 50, International Food Policy Research Institute, Ethiopia Strategy Support Program (ESSP), Addis Ababa.

World Bank. 2020a. *World Development Report 2020: Trading for Development in the Age of Global Value Chains.* Washington, DC: World Bank. https://www.worldbank.org /en/publication/wdr2020.

World Bank. 2020b. World Development Indicators (database). https://databank.world bank.org/source/world-development-indicators.

Wrigley, N., D. Warm, B. Margetts, and A. Whelan. 2002. "Assessing the Impact of Improved Retail Access on Diet in a 'Food Desert': A Preliminary Report." *Urban Studies* 39 (11): 2061–82.

Chapter 2

Access to Food: The Role of Physical Infrastructure in Abidjan, Rabat, and Niamey

In food markets, as in any market, matching supply with demand is the main problem. However, food markets differ in three significant ways. First, well-functioning food markets are essential for consumers' survival, or at least their well-being. Second, the physical distance between farmers and consumers requires massive investments in infrastructure. And, third, the products traded in food markets are perishable and need to be sold quickly. These three differences justify the need for donors and municipalities to pay extra attention to existing market infrastructure, identify its shortcomings, and find ways to remedy them.

The Role of Infrastructure in Matching Supply with Demand

Physical Market Infrastructure: A Major Role in Ensuring Food and Nutrition Security

Chapter 1 showed the extent of national and global changes that affect food systems. This chapter raises the question of how public development policies in Africa can address these changes through physical market infrastructure, which includes "hard" food supply and distribution infrastructure such as roads, markets, storage, and refrigerated trucks. (Chapter 3 discusses policy design for nonphysical "soft" institutional market infrastructure, such as price and quality information systems, contract enforcement mechanisms, and access to credit.)

This chapter begins by discussing two important questions:

- How can physical market infrastructure provide food and nutrition security to meet the four criteria defined at the 1996 World Food Summit: availability, quality, stability, and accessibility (FAO 1996)? Market infrastructure plays a major role in achieving these technical and economic criteria. For example, quality pertains to both hygiene and consumer preferences. Access and availability imply that food is affordable for everyone.

- To what extent does market infrastructure directly affect the United Nations Sustainable Development Goals (SDGs) such as poverty eradication, job creation, and urban and national sustainability?

The Importance of Geographical Context as Reflected in Three Descriptive Case Studies

Although the physical market infrastructure in Abidjan, Rabat, and Niamey shares a common objective, it operates quite differently in each city. This chapter illustrates how it responds to the previous two questions along the entire logistics chain, from the moment products leave farm sites until they reach the consumer (without going into the big issue of supporting agricultural and food production in developing countries). The rapid pace of economic and social change in developing countries has often overtaken market infrastructure, with profound consequences at all levels.

On the supply side, these changes have led to pushing urban and suburban production far outside cities. Does this affect cities' food supply? Does greater distance require more intermediaries or more management infrastructure? On the demand side, what are the logistics of managing intraurban, rural, and imported food flows? How can consumers continue to have a stable, diversified, and affordable supply of foodstuffs? At each level, physical market infrastructure must solve logistical issues by, for example, including unloading docks, cold storage equipment, and other facilities. It must also solve economic issues by, for example, allowing price formation and the observation of product quality.

An Analytical Approach to Public Policy Design

This chapter also examines a third question: What should public authorities and their technical and financial partners do to promote and support effective market infrastructure? The answer requires understanding which variables and conditions matter to food system actors. The tools available for making policy decisions have vastly different effects, depending on market structure. In particular, one must sharply distinguish between the tools available in the short term and those available in the medium term. Short-term tools do not require investments in infrastructure and generally concern price and quantity regulation, such as quotas or subsidies for prices, transport, or land purchases. Medium-term tools require infrastructure investment, such as building a road or a marketplace. In the short term, market structure, particularly the location of producers and existing market infrastructure, is a given. The main policy lever is price, via subsidies or taxes. In the medium term, market conditions can be changed by reducing transport costs or by reestablishing competition in a given market. Therefore, this chapter focuses on the spatial and physical aspects of market infrastructure. Economic theory drawn from geographical economics is used to understand how transport costs, product perishability, and demand influence the location of producers and commercial infrastructure, and how producers and marketplaces can be used to achieve the SDGs.

Chapter 2 Contents

These three questions are answered in the three sections that follow. The first analyzes producer behavior, such as the long-term choice of production location, and levers that reduce the cost of market access, following Von Thünen's (1826) classic analysis of how the city influences producer location through transport costs. It also covers producers' short-term marketing choices, such as whether to bring production to market, by addressing production consolidation issues and wholesale market centralization, among other factors. The second section focuses on consumer and distributor decision-making. How do consumers decide what food to consume and where to purchase it? How do distributors locate in the medium term according to this demand? How are consumers affected by distributors' choices? How can public policy affect these choices in the short or medium term? The third section reviews possible public policy actions and addresses governance and implementation issues. It examines policy actions in terms of "what" and "how": What normative recommendations does economic theory propose? And what do the three case studies reveal about governance structures? The three case studies provide practitioners with an analytical framework they can use to identify valid recommendations and actors who can implement them.

From Producers to Market Infrastructure: The Effects of Globalization and Urbanization on Rural and Urban Lands

Since the time of human settlement and urbanization, cities and the farms that feed them have been intertwined, marked by spatial, economic, and political relationships. Scott (2019) offers an illustration from one of the earliest city-states, the Sumerian city of Uruk, in what is now southern Iraq. Even before the appearance of the first states, urban elites set up political and religious institutions and physical infrastructure such as canals, roads, and silos to ensure that populated areas would receive food.

The industrial revolutions of the 19th and 20th centuries reinforced this trend. William Cronon's (1991) monumental history of Chicago reveals how the city's creation, growth, and apogee were made possible by the rich plains that surrounded it (Cronon 2019). It also describes how these plains determined the city's agricultural choices. Cronon illustrates the complexity of physical market infrastructure that relies on marketplaces as well as transport infrastructure, particularly railways and canals, and commodity storage and trading technologies, such as elevators and grain silos.

Urban and Suburban Producers: Persisting Despite Everything

Cities can simultaneously attract some activities and repel others. What structuring forces explain agents' decisions and thus the location of farms in relation to cities? According to economic theory, centralizing and centrifugal forces structure these decisions (Calmette, forthcoming). Production costs, which are higher in cities, where land and labor are often more expensive, are usually centrifugal, meaning they push production away from cities. Transport costs, which include direct costs and—even more important—costs related to product perishability, are usually centralizing, meaning they pull agricultural production closer to cities. Production costs, returns to scale, transport costs, and perishability will thus move the production of a given product closer to or farther away from the consumer. In this way, urbanization and globalization have important effects on physical market infrastructure through factors such as transport costs, returns to scale, and demand, thereby modifying these centrifugal and centralizing forces and transforming territories and the food system.

The Relationship between Perishability and Proximity

In Sub-Saharan Africa, the symbiotic relationship between city and country is just as strong as it was in Uruk or Chicago, especially because African cities have seen the rapid growth mentioned in chapter 1. The German economist Von Thünen (1826) modeled this symbiotic relationship using only commodity transport costs. Unlike Ricardo, Von Thünen assumes constant agricultural yields, which means that the presence of a city (understood as a market of consumers) and transport costs are the sole geographical variations. Von Thünen's analysis as summarized by Calmette (forthcoming) finds that crops with the highest transport costs—especially the most perishable crops such as fruits and other market garden produce—tend to be grown closer to the city center. Then come the less perishable crops such as grains and processed products that can be imported from different parts of the world. However, live animals, fresh meat, fish and poultry, and frozen products are extremely difficult to ship in the absence of suitable infrastructure. Therefore, the relationship between perishability and proximity is stronger when transport infrastructure is old, especially if it lacks refrigeration capacity. Frozen chicken can be imported from China, but it is quite expensive to bring fresh chicken meat to Niamey from the Nigerien countryside.

The cases of Abidjan and Niamey illustrate how transport costs and perishability structure markets near urban consumers. For example, Koffie-Bikpo and Adaye (2014) list 312 market gardeners in the city of Abidjan, while farmers in the subprefecture of Bonoua, located about 60 kilometers from Abidjan, specialize in cassava, which is less perishable than fruits and other vegetables. In Niamey, urban vegetable crops are varied, even though the average farm size is smaller than that of the farms around Abidjan. Andres and Lebailly (2012) estimate that 43 percent of Niamey's urban population practiced at least one form of agriculture in 2008. Suburban areas, too, host a large share of rice farms, fisheries, market gardens, and fruit orchards.

Poultry, milk animals, and other livestock are also raised on urban farms. Such farms are concentrated along the Niger River to serve Niamey and thus save on overland transport costs. Nationally grown grains and large ruminants mainly supply the capital. Maps 2.1 and 2.2 illustrate production areas and distribution flows for tomatoes and millet, which have far different perishability. Proximity is important for tomatoes because they are highly perishable and require fast and efficient routes to market in the absence of refrigerated transport services. Therefore, tomato growers located within 50 kilometers of Niamey directly supply the city's markets, including growers in a "vegetable belt" that encircles the city limits. In the dry season, when tomatoes cannot be grown domestically, Niger imports them from neighboring Burkina Faso, Benin, and Nigeria. Recently, imports from Morocco have also appeared, thanks in part to better refrigerated transport services. A highly perishable leafy vegetable, moringa, has seen its popularity grow in Niger. Like tomatoes, it mainly comes from the Niamey vegetable belt.

By contrast, millet, a dry, relatively easily shipped and stored product, has more distant and diverse origins. It accounts for about 80 percent of grain production because it is well adapted to the Sahelian climate. Three neighboring countries—Mali, Nigeria, and Burkina Faso—are the largest suppliers of millet to Niger. These imports largely pass through informal channels because of Niger's long and poorly controlled borders, contributing to the structure of relationships between producers and consumers.

Chicken is an intermediate case between tomatoes and millet in terms of perishability. Meat chickens are raised largely in Niamey; in fact, 40 percent of the chicken consumed comes from urban growers. Most poultry is raised for personal consumption or sold live directly to consumers through informal channels. Niger also imports frozen chicken from nearby and distant sources, including Nigeria, Burkina Faso, Brazil, and various European countries.

Map 2.1 Tomato Flows to Niamey

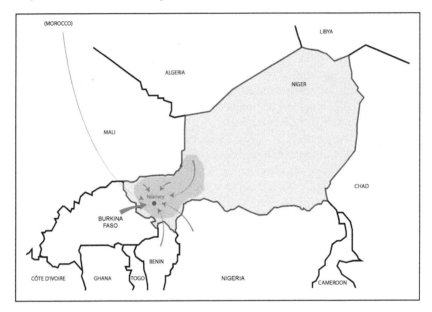

Source: D'Angelo and Brisson 2019.

Map 2.2 Millet Flows to Niamey

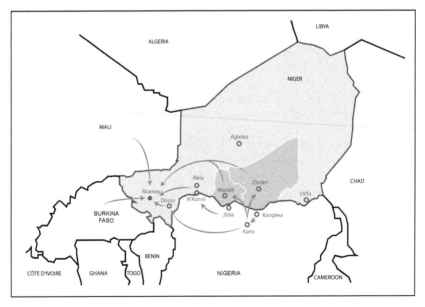

Source: D'Angelo and Brisson 2019.

Regardless of product origin, the ability of market infrastructure to provide ongoing supplies of foodstuffs strongly affects prices. Tomatoes, for example, are extremely seasonal. In Niger, locally grown tomatoes are available only between January and April. They are largely absent during the dry season from May to July until the supply rises slightly between August and December. This seasonality causes large fluctuations in price and availability that threaten household food security and nutrition. Although Niger is a special case, large fluctuations in price, quality, and availability occur relatively frequently in Sahelian countries, and they will likely increase with the effects of climate change (FAO et al. 2018). Therefore, national and transnational infrastructure that can ensure regular supplies of foodstuffs is essential, particularly storage facilities.

Urbanization—Driving Out Some Producers and Crops

Perishability alone does not determine where producers locate farms; some centrifugal forces also play a role. Agriculture competes for land with other productive sectors and residential uses. Higher prices for real estate reduce the relative advantage of proximity. Pollution also plays a role. When regulation is lacking, polluting manufacturing activities sometimes are located close to farmland, thereby reducing the latter's productivity and quality. Such occurrences do not, however, invalidate Von Thünen's analysis of rents; the analysis just needs to integrate the fact that the higher productivity and revenues associated with urban activities lead to land being reallocated.

In Morocco, Rabat's development illustrates the higher cost of locating farms close to urban areas. Map 2.3 depicts how urban growth pushed the old vegetable-growing areas of Témara farther outward. When land markets were deregulated during a liberalization wave in the 1990s, this pushing-out effect grew even stronger because residential real estate began to replace agricultural land. However, the most fragile crops that would cost the most to ship remain locally grown. For example, local farms still produce 33 percent of coriander, lettuce, and mint, with the most distant coming from Morocco's economic capital, Casablanca, 120 kilometers away. However, other proximity-sensitive market garden vegetable crops are gradually being pushed out at a projected pace of 4,500 hectares per year until 2025 (Valette and Philifert 2014). Market gardening, no longer profitable in the city, generates profits in other regions, such as the Souss region (550 kilometers from Rabat) and Doukkala (260 kilometers from Rabat).

Today, nearby demand counts less than soil quality in a farm's value. When transport infrastructure allows it, perishability and closeness to consumers matter less to farm location than do production conditions. For example, the coastal region of Agadir has become the main source of fruits and vegetables for Rabat, particularly tomatoes (map 2.3). By contrast, potatoes are produced on farms closer to the city,[1] whereas citrus comes from various areas.

Map 2.3 Produce Flows to Rabat

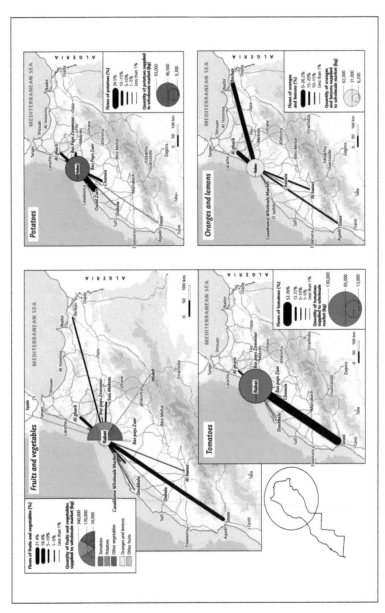

Source: Aderghal, Lemeilleur, and Romagny 2019. Map created by Aderghal and illustrated by A. Binance in the Tourism, Heritage, and Sustainable Land Development Engineering Lab of the Life Sciences and Letters Faculty of Mohammed V University in Rabat.

In the case of Abidjan, local production remains important, as Von Thünen's model predicted and as noted earlier. Côte d'Ivoire saw a decline because of political crises in the 2000s, which were followed recently by an economic rebound. A similar cycle affected agricultural production; during the 2000–2010 political crises, market gardens developed strongly, while other economic opportunities declined. These trends reversed once rapid growth resumed in Côte d'Ivoire. Oura (2012) believes that farms within Abidjan's city limits will eventually disappear as farmland is converted to residential or commercial use and that urban sprawl will reduce suburban agriculture. Pollution can also strongly limit urban farming. According to Andres and Lebailly (2012), because of the pollution in Niamey neighborhoods where industrial activities are located, gardens and orchards cannot be established there.

Globalization—Prompting New Approaches to Agricultural Spaces

The observations just made are as true at the international level as at the national one. Krugman (1980) has shown the importance of the variable "access to markets" in international trade. Nearby demand is important in the presence of transport costs, but when transport costs decline and demand becomes international, production costs dominate producers' choice of location, especially when higher demand leads to economies of scale and production volumes increase. Thus Morocco increased tomato exports by nearly 75 percent in 10 years, becoming the world's fifth-largest tomato exporter as large farms moved away from urban areas. Tomato growers selected various Moroccan regions for specialization and made the specific investments needed for exports. They divided their lands, devoting some to seasonal local crops cultivated in fields, some to greenhouse crops, and some to crops for food processors.

Exports have become one of Morocco's major markets. In 2010 the country exported one-third of all its tomatoes, green beans, zucchini, and other fruits and vegetables, 96 percent of which went to the European Union (IMIST 2011). In the face of such external demand, hydrological and geological features drive the choice of production location. Agricultural areas move toward specializing in high-demand products for the domestic or international markets. Nationally, the trend runs toward higher fruit and vegetable production, bolstered by the use of greenhouses, which allow private operators to supply markets more easily on a regular basis.

In Niger, production for export also plays a significant role, particularly for fresh chilis and onions, the two main agricultural exports. Niamey plays an important role in marketing these products in addition to serving as a logistics platform, despite the city having insufficient facilities and an overconcentration of commercial activities in the urban center. International demand has transformed domestic production in turn, affecting the national food supply and distribution infrastructure, including farming areas, transport infrastructure, and logistics chains. Distant production areas have led to stronger and longer-distance distribution channels and an increase in the number of intermediaries.

Figure 2.1 Centrifugal and Centralizing Forces Affecting Farms: Côte d'Ivoire, Morocco, and Niger

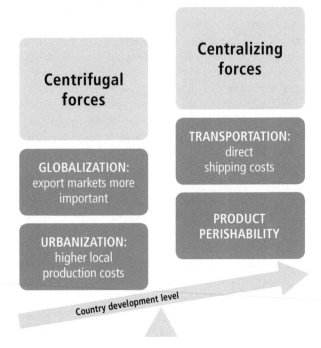

Source: AFD study team.
Note: Centralizing forces diminish as a country's development level rises.

It is important that policy makers understand that trade globalization and lower international transport costs affect both export goods and domestic trade because economic forces determine regional specializations. These changes took place simultaneously with trade liberalization and especially urban land deregulation, which made it possible to transform farmland and orchards into houses and other uses. In summary, in the three cities and countries studied it appears that centrifugal forces, more vigorous than centralizing forces (figure 2.1), result in a fairly standard distribution of crops located either close to the city, on national lands, or grown abroad, depending on the country's development level and therefore its effective demand and market infrastructure (table 2.1).

Table 2.1 Food Product Origins: Abidjan, Rabat, and Niamey

	Mainly imported products	Mainly domestic products	Mainly locally grown products
Abidjan	Rice, fish, meat, milk	Cassava and grains	Seasonal vegetables, poultry
Rabat	Grains (wheat, corn, barley)	Tomatoes, citrus fruits, potatoes, livestock	Lettuces, mint, other herbs
Niamey	Rice, other dry grains, root vegetables, flours, oils, sugar	Grains	Market garden crops, fruit and nut trees, rice, livestock

Source: AFD study team, based on the country case studies listed in box 1.1.

From Producers to Retailers: Intermediaries and Wholesale Markets

Food chain intermediaries have also had to permanently change their work practices to adapt to the remoteness of food production areas. This section explores why these changes have occurred, focusing on the trade among producers, collectors, and wholesalers. It describes market infrastructure components in detail and explains why infrastructure is located in certain places, describing its fundamental role in routing foodstuffs to cities. As described in this section, the three case studies provide highly variable answers to such questions. The last section discusses relationships between retail and other consumer markets, focusing on the "last mile" problem.

Defining Market Infrastructure

Physical market infrastructure can be defined as all the buildings, facilities, and equipment used to ship, consolidate, store, and trade foodstuffs. Markets include components such as stalls, stall roofs, loading bays, refrigeration facilities, and warehouses. These components vary from city to city and within cities. According to economic theory, wholesale markets and their infrastructure are impure public goods, close to club or toll goods. In their desirable characteristics of nonexcludable and nonrivalrous, wholesale markets resemble public goods, but congestion effects limit their use. Physical market infrastructure also includes small retail shops that sell more easily stored goods such as rice, flour, canned food, and condiments. Large supermarkets are also important links in the food supply chain. They usually operate relatively autonomously from intermediaries because producers often supply supermarkets directly for the sake of maintaining verifiable quality—a supply chain management system known as vertical integration. The choice of infrastructure type therefore depends on the type of product, consumer demand, and other factors.

Figure 2.2 shows the logistics of food supply and distribution. In the first step, trader-collector drivers buy products from producers. In some relatively rare cases in the three cities studied, farmers bring their production directly to a wholesale market or open-air unloading area. In the second step, a wholesale market centralizes trade between the intermediaries who collect products from either distant producers or import-export agents in the case of imported products. The wholesale market's size, facilities, and location (distance from producers and city) determine whom it serves and which products it sells. When a wholesale market centralizes a large share of commodities, the market plays the role of a "city" in Von Thünen's sense inasmuch as products are organized around it. This gives proximity to wholesale markets its value. The wholesale market sets up various distinct product areas for intermediaries that supply retail markets, restaurants, supermarkets, neighborhood stores, microretailers, and others.

If municipal regulations do not determine distributor types, wholesale markets exist on a continuum that runs from large markets that are more centralized, have more facilities, and bring together more sellers and buyers, to atomized, smaller, open-air markets with smaller sellers and buyers. In other words, food distribution centers range from extremely centralized, where the congestion costs are greater than the benefits of the built infrastructure, to totally dispersed with lower-quality or no infrastructure. The actors involved on different scales can also be classified along a continuum. Large wholesale markets tend to gather wholesalers and trader-collector drivers who obtain products from producers and sell to large retailers and restaurants, although sometimes large wholesale markets supply small retailers, microretailers, and even consumers.

Figure 2.2 **Simplified Food Distribution System**

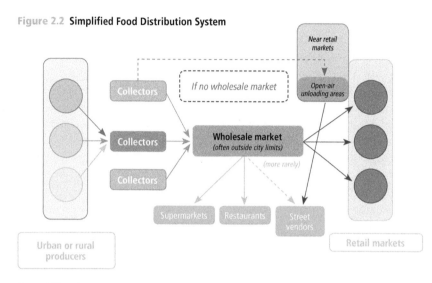

Source: AFD study team.

The Importance of Intermediaries

Intermediaries provide a matching service in exchange for a commission. The size of their markup makes it possible to evaluate the efficiency of a market. As production locations change, how do intermediaries reposition themselves vis-à-vis the food supply and distribution infrastructure? To understand the factors influencing their decisions, it may be helpful to recall the theory of market matching (see Calmette, forthcoming, for a theoretical presentation). In theory, a market is "perfect" when the sales price equals the purchase price plus transport costs. However, the friction between the producer and consumer makes this situation unrealistic. All the infrastructure and actors operating between the producer and consumer—the physical distance, wholesale seller to retail seller, information about quality, etc.—generate costs and margins that can make the difference between market infrastructure that does or does not work.

In theory, it is easy to measure matching efficiency; it is the difference between the price paid to the producer and the price paid by the consumer minus the cost of transport and intermediation. In practice, however, it is hard to calculate. How do you know whether the margins and prices charged by intermediaries simply reflect the cost of an efficient system or reflect either inefficiencies or margins inflated by monopoly positions? This question has generated much literature on market integration (Brunelin and Portugal-Perez 2013).

Here, the focus is on the role of intermediaries and their market power. Intermediaries play a crucial role by enabling trade and influencing its cost. Often, an increasing return to scale effect drives the concentration of trading activity, justifying the use of centralized markets rather than using purely seller-to-consumer matching (Fafchamps, Gabre-Madhin, and Minten 2005). This raises an economic question: How can markets generate increasing returns, while avoiding the monopolization of rents by intermediaries that become too powerful? Moreover, Fafchamps and Hill (2005) show that intermediaries can also change the composition of supply: more efficient intermediaries will allow marginal producers to participate in the market. In other words, in the short and medium term all intermediaries along the distribution chain will have a decisive effect on producer revenues, choice of markets and products, and so forth. Intermediaries also determine the accessibility of products for consumers in terms of distance and cost.

Physical Distance and Number of Intermediaries

The question of producers' distance to retail markets and the configuration of intermediaries is important because proximity tends to reduce the number of intermediaries (Lemeilleur et al. 2019), the distance of information flows, and the extent of infrastructure and capital investments needed. Short distribution chains tend to reduce, but not eliminate, many actors because urban producers, like rural ones, tend to be dispersed. Producers are also often uncertain about land ownership rights, which reinforce power asymmetries (see next section). More distant farms require more logistics and intermediaries. In the case of Côte d'Ivoire, a study by Camara (2016) illustrates the problem. Leaf spinach, the most fragile product, is grown within city limits and requires only one or two intermediaries, whereas tomatoes are grown 300 kilometers away from cities, or 600 kilometers away out of season, and require three or four inter-mediaries (graph 2.1). The next section looks at where intermediaries locate in cities.

Graph 2.1 **Number of Intermediaries by Farms' Distance to City**

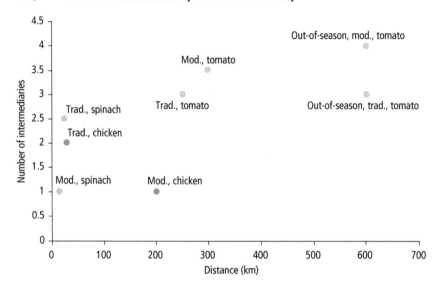

Source: Camara 2016.

Note: Mod. = modern distribution circuit; trad. = traditional distribution circuit.

Location in the City

In Sub-Saharan Africa in general, managing rapid urbanization despite limited administrative capacity has posed a fundamental problem (Tollens 1997). In the absence of official administrators, informal actors have supplied the ever-increasing urban demand without municipal authorities centralizing food market functions. In Côte d'Ivoire and Niger, municipalities have not designated areas for specific types of food sales, with mixed effects. In Rabat, municipal regulations require vegetables to be sold through wholesale markets (figure 2.3).

The use of private arrangements to create wholesale markets has some advantages. For example, retailers can immediately access wholesalers, which creates trusting relationships and provides access to a wide variety of products. Conversely, trade decentralization has several negative consequences. For example, a wholesale market's increasing returns to scale are not captured, which curbs investment in needed facilities. Nor does decentralization allow information to be shared upstream on the producer end because use of telephones impairs effective information aggregation. Decentralization also tends to further congest overloaded urban infrastructure and limits the ability of under-staffed or ill-equipped health agencies to carry out inspections.

Figure 2.3 **Wholesale and Retail Market Configurations**

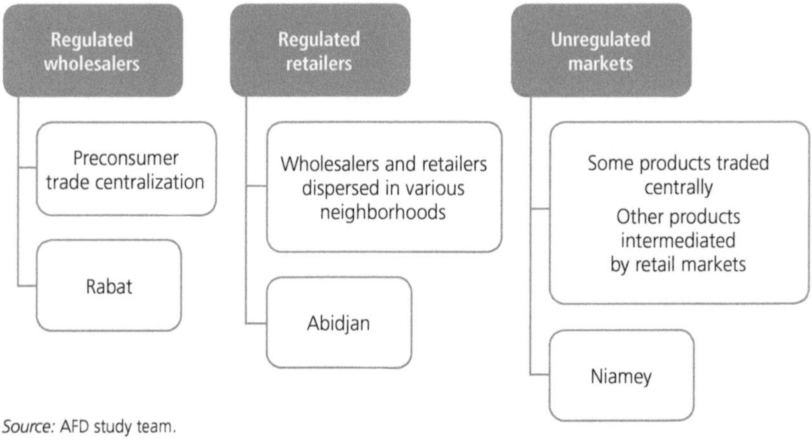

Regulated wholesalers	Regulated retailers	Unregulated markets
Preconsumer trade centralization	Wholesalers and retailers dispersed in various neighborhoods	Some products traded centrally Other products intermediated by retail markets
Rabat	Abidjan	Niamey

Source: AFD study team.

Abidjan, having no centralized wholesale market, is an extreme case (Harre 2001). Despite the city's population growth, its commercial sector has not built the infrastructure needed for urban sprawl. Harre (2001) finds that the national government did not make enough land available in Abidjan for a centralized wholesale market, despite requests from wholesalers. Most *grands marchés* (large central markets) therefore increasingly resemble the open-air unloading areas near retail markets, where sellers and buyers route products and negotiate prices. These distribution areas are popular and have high economic potential. Usually located just outside the city center or on highways, they attract consumers from all over the city. Some grands marchés are equipped with built structures, electrical connections, and water service. Trader-collector drivers source products from rural or urban producers and route products to the open-air unloading areas or distribution centers located near retail markets. The trader-collectors negotiate prices and volumes, often by telephone or through their relationships. For example, the yam market (described by Mahyao 2008) substitutes information shared by telephone for the physical matching of supply with demand; wholesalers deal with brokers from yam farm regions who take care of logistics. In this way, yams, a fragile vegetable likely to lose quality during transport breaks, can be quickly traded.

In Niamey, market arrangements also dominate public policy decisions, but they produce the opposite effect. All wholesale activities are concentrated in the city center. The Grand Marché features imported food wholesalers. Katako is the market for grain, tubers, and fruits, and the Petit Marché (Small Market) serves as the delivery area for local produce and other local products.

A few wholesale activities have moved to the periphery, such as sellers of sugarcane, onions, and other produce, as well as wholesalers who moved there following a fire in the Petit Marché. Fruit and vegetable supply chains are often shorter and simpler than others. They also tend to involve fewer intermediaries than products with longer shelf lives. Map 2.4 illustrates Niamey's wholesale distribution scheme and its relationship to retail markets. Its centralized, extreme concentration generates additional costs because of the longer transport times for trader-collector drivers, wholesalers, and retailers. It also affects the market on the consumer end. Centralization attracts retail consumers to the wholesale markets, reducing the distinction between wholesale and retail. Such a market also creates negative externalities, such as traffic congestion in the city center both day and night, excessive use of water and electricity, noise pollution, and other nuisances.

Map 2.4 **Intermarket Distribution of Fresh and Dried Products, Niamey**

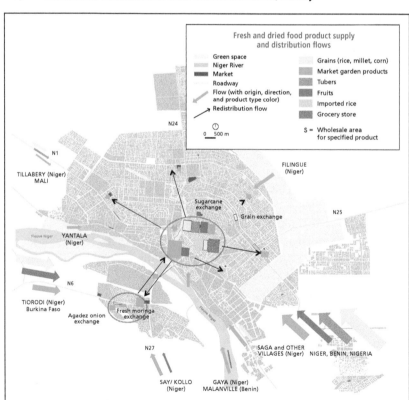

Source: D'Angelo and Brisson 2019.

Map 2.5 **Fresh Fruit and Vegetable Flows from Wholesale Markets in Rabat and Salé to Retail Markets**

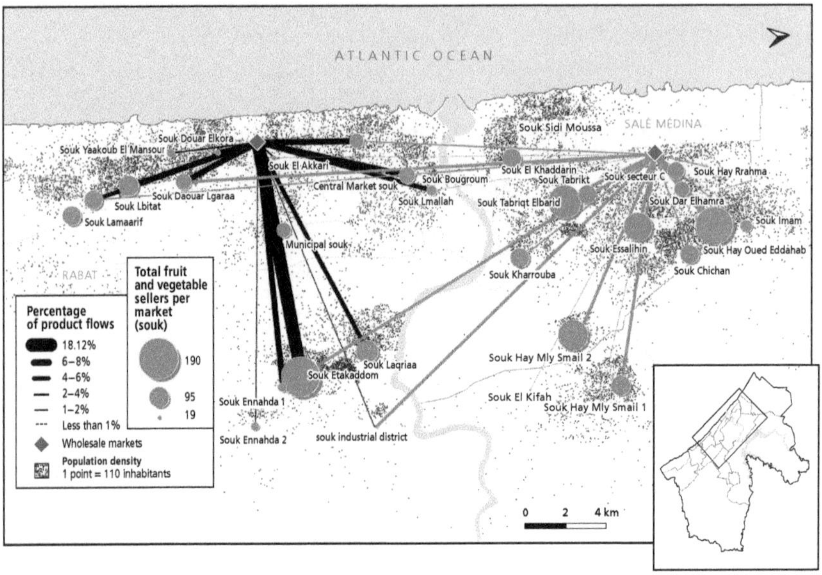

Source: Aderghal, Lemeilleur, and Romagny 2019. Map created by Aderghal and illustrated by A. Binance in the Tourism, Heritage, and Sustainable Land Development Engineering Lab of the Life Sciences and Letters Faculty of the Mohammed V University, Rabat.
Note: Conic projection conforms with the zone Lambert Nord Maroc.

Rabat is an intermediate case. Regulators have given wholesale markets a particularly important role—regulations dictate that fruits and vegetables must pass through urban wholesale markets (map 2.5). This explains why wholesalers that sell products that do not fall under this regulation, such as mint or chicken, also use these markets. However, 30–50 percent of products subject to the regulation circumvent it, bypassing the urban markets. The regulations were intended to organize the market and to allow the authorities to carry out health and safety inspections. Beyond bolstering the efficiency and sustainability of food supply and distribution infrastructure, however, the regulations also aim to allow the government to levy taxes on transactions. Thus localities often perceive regulated markets as major contributors to public resources, whether or not they actually are, as discussed shortly.

Regulated wholesale markets are in Rabat, Salé, and Témara. A fourth unregulated wholesale market is located in the municipality of Bouknadel. These marketplaces compete through their product offerings, infrastructure quality, and transaction tax rates. The latter vary according to volume, ranging from 1.5 percent to 7 percent in the regulated markets, but running much lower in unregulated Bouknadel. Souks also compete with wholesale markets. Thus even when regulations require fruits and vegetables to be sold through the three central wholesale markets, competition from informal sellers must be taken into account.

This long-running situation and a lack of maintenance has resulted in outdated facilities. In Salé, the wholesale market—established in 1956, the oldest in the city—has only the most rudimentary infrastructure. It lacks, for example, refrigerated storage. Because of its historical location, it also handles the largest volume of foodstuffs. In light of its aging infrastructure, the authorities built two new wholesale markets, one in Rabat in 1974 and another in Témara in 2005. The new markets have better facilities, particularly refrigerated storage areas (Valyans Consulting 2010, cited in Rousseau, Boyet, and Harroud 2019).They also have a reputation for better-quality products. The Rabat wholesale market features meat, fish, and poultry products, as well as a slaughterhouse and a grain exchange. Between 10 and 35 percent of its products are locally grown. Conversely, the Bouknadel market has no permanent built structure. It is mostly used by local producers whose sales account for 80 percent of the products sold. More important, regulated wholesalers are the dominant sellers, accounting for 50 percent of sales in Témara and 73 percent in Salé.

Wholesale markets have three advantages, as illustrated by Abidjan, Rabat, and Niamey:

- Wholesalers can sort products and then charge more for higher-quality items (Chen and Stamoulis 2012), incentivizing producers to improve quality in turn so they, too, will receive higher prices. Without these incentives, the theory of adverse selection predicts lower product quality (see chapter 3). In Rabat, multiple wholesale outlets provide these incentives.

- Because the equilibrium price stabilizes with larger volumes, centralizing trade allows vertical scaling and economies of scale.

- Wholesale markets allow horizontal scaling through greater product diversification. Thus concentration effects explain why traders in Rabat choose to sell in the wholesale markets products that are not required to be sold through those markets.

The case of Rabat also illustrates the limits of wholesale trade regulation. Since the 2000s, when distribution chains became more complicated, traders have negatively perceived the requirement to sell through wholesale markets to be a way of slowing down agreements that could be made mutually. In addition, market infrastructure must offer the benefits needed to be more attractive than the competing informal sellers. Because wholesale markets match supply and demand, generating a balance in which all actors turn to a wholesale market is complicated because participants must be convinced that others will also use it. The advantages of wholesale markets are maximized when products can be shipped to the city and when urban wholesale markets can provide a crucial, direct link to retailers. Policies for urban markets must take a city's future growth into account and choose a sufficiently distant location in order to allow for future market extensions.

Market Infrastructure and Consumers' Access to Food

The Urban Economy and Consumer Access

Product distributors choose among various locations based on demand density, product variety, and customer purchasing capacity; their own transport costs (as noted earlier); and their competitive strategy. In turn, these choices influence consumers' abilities to access a healthy, varied diet at reasonable prices. Policy makers may thus envisage building a marketplace or other urban facility in the medium or long term. In the short term, however, such a policy is unlikely to affect any of the variables just described. Instead, public authorities can act indirectly on, for example, transportation costs, or directly on prices and quantities. However, to imagine and plan for the likely effects of such policies, policy makers need to understand consumers' and producers' decision variables to avoid possible adverse effects.

Consumers do not necessarily capture efficiency gains, which essentially depend on the price elasticity of demand (see Calmette, forthcoming, for more details). Such gains also depend on how consumer transportation costs affect the cost of accessing food. What follows is a look at how consumers choose among price, quality, variety, and proximity. Geographical economics illuminates distributor strategies for determining location and pricing and can therefore guide public policy makers. For example, opening one retail market close to another one can lead to greater competition and lower prices, but it can also lead to inefficient price wars. Hotelling (1929) was the first to explore the link between location choice and price differentiation. When seller location is a given, the result is simple: the distance to other sellers increases the market power of each and therefore the price for the consumers. When sellers choose their location, they face two effects: moving closer to a central point can capture a larger market, but doing so intensifies price competition. Under certain hypotheses, the second effect dominates, which means that sellers prefer to segment the market and keep prices as high as possible. In this view, distance is a form of friction that prevents price competition and makes consumers captives. Two opposite cases illustrate the tension between these two views of location effects: a centralized marketplace with high competition and low prices, or a dispersed, almost monopolistic market with higher prices.

In a market that has monopolistic effects, an important distinction must be drawn between price excluding transport costs (pricing known in international trade as free on board, FOB) and price including transport costs (pricing known as cost, insurance, and freight, CIF)—see Calmette (forthcoming). CIF pricing assumes that a supplier can charge consumers prices that vary according to their distance from the market. Although this pricing is unlikely in a centralized market, itinerant sellers may have enough information about their customers and bargaining power to adjust prices according to customer location. By contrast, a seller's FOB pricing strategy sets a price in order to maximize profit over a market area. Beyond this area, direct and indirect transport costs are too high for consumers. In both cases, any drop in transport costs is reflected differently, depending on distance: FOB fully reflects transport cost in the seller's market area, while only part of the transport cost is passed on with CIF.

Reaching Conclusions from These Models

Consumers located far from market areas will often pay more for food, and they will prefer a more informal product offer tailored to their distant location, such as that offered by microretailers. Studies of the United Kingdom (such as Whelan et al. 2002) and India (Rao 2000) find that the poorest prefer to pay more and buy near their location. A policy that reduces consumer transportation costs only partially benefits the poor because the seller will capture some of the reduction. Near market areas, the result of a transportation policy depends on the structure of competition. In a monopoly situation, the seller could capture gains created through transportation subsidies, but in a competitive situation proximity would reduce prices. These findings are important: they suggest that different types of offers are complementary, and that customers located far from markets (who are often the poorest) will pay a higher price and only partially benefit from subsidized transportation costs.

A policy may have distinct effects on consumers and suppliers, in addition to affecting near-to or far-from market customers differently. Who receives the benefit of subsidized shipping or transport? It depends on the price elasticity of demand and on supply compared with the price. Demand elasticity greater than 1 leads to an increase in demand from the producer that is greater than the cost reduction. The producer surplus also increases. When demand elasticity is less than 1, the effect is ambiguous in aggregated terms. Customers react to a drop in transport costs and increase demand, which will increase prices, especially if supply is inelastic. Therefore, food security, particularly in neighborhoods with smaller supplies, crucially depends on the ability to increase supply elasticity, which often depends in turn on local conditions, such as market structure and vehicle availability. Policy makers must take such factors into account.

Interactions between consumer and producer capital investments can also lessen the efficiency of some public interventions. For example, Lagakos (2016) finds that supermarkets realize productivity gains because of economies of scale and efficient logistics. However, supermarkets achieve such gains only when a majority of consumers have access to a car, a situation not necessarily replicable in an underdeveloped country. More generally, consumers choose market infrastructure that suits them. For example, a consumer without a refrigerator will probably make frequent shopping trips and will therefore prefer to buy perishable products from nearby shops or itinerant vendors rather than from supermarkets, even though the latter offer greater quantities at a lower cost. In summary, the theories just described lead to important predictions about the effects of policies that promote access to food: the ability of consumers to capture transportation cost subsidies will vary, depending on their distance to the market and whether the market is competitive or monopolistic. Similarly, these subsidies will increase consumer or producer welfare according to the price elasticity of supply or demand. For more details and theoretical discussions, see Calmette (forthcoming).

Consumer Preferences: Price, Proximity, and Quality
Because consumer preferences matter when modeling public policy interventions, researchers surveyed consumers in Abidjan, Rabat, and Niamey. The surveys asked consumers where they preferred to purchase food based on three criteria:

- **Price.** Price, understood as affordability, is an essential component of access to food. In urban Sub-Saharan Africa, food represents between 15 percent (South Africa) and 60 percent (Democratic Republic of Congo) of household spending, averaging 47 percent (World Bank 2010). Thus price is an important criterion for the consumer. It turns out that food is 30–40 percent more expensive in Africa based on the per capita gross domestic product (GDP) than in the rest of the world (Allen 2017). Barriers to international trade and lower productivity contribute to the expense, as does the food distribution system. As a result, households give priority to finding the lowest-cost food sources.

- **Quality.** Product quality covers many dimensions. First, it ensures that a product will not harm health. Hygienic storage and transport conditions are essential (see chapter 3 for a review of the conditions through which information sharing helps to maintain quality). Second, the place of purchase plays an important role. Quality includes the buying experience. Comfortable surroundings and a preexisting relationship with the seller serve as consumer amenities. They also indirectly communicate information about the products. Thus different markets present vertical product differentiation.

- **Proximity.** Proximity is understood in both an economic and a geographical sense. The cost of travel time depends on the existence of public or private transportation, its cost, and its disutility. In particular, the higher the underemployment rate, the lower is the opportunity cost of time.

These preferences inform consumers' price elasticity. The weight consumers give each variable affects distributors' strategic pricing decisions. For example, if proximity is the most important criterion, stores can increase prices and take advantage of their "captive" clientele. If customers prefer lower prices over proximity, price competition can intensify. All of this, of course, depends on a city's form and the quality of its transportation infrastructure. Consumer surveys in the three cases studied illustrate how much consumer choice gives contrasting results, depending on constraints such as income and transportation, among others.[2]

Consumers surveyed in Abidjan said they have a strong preference for proximity. They counted variety as a distant second, and price took third place. Only 8 percent of respondents mentioned quality-related issues. However, if respondents citing the quality of products and the quality of the buying experience are added together, 21 percent of respondents prefer quality. In Niamey, the comparison is incomplete because only 70 consumers were surveyed, and so the findings provide only a qualitative indication. Nevertheless, Niamey respondents revealed that a significant portion of people buy food on a daily basis. Because they lack the means to preserve food, they must make frequent purchases, which affects distributors' choice of sales outlet location. Affordability and quality motivate their choice of marketplace, while distance trails as a factor. In Rabat, higher incomes have prompted consumer demand for better-quality products, but distance remains an important criterion. The gradual arrival of supermarkets and the development of modern food distribution channels has segmented consumers into those who have supermarkets nearby, with higher-quality products and prices, and those who live in neighborhoods with fewer or smaller markets.

The consumer preferences triangle is configured differently in each city, leading to different allocations of infrastructure and policy recommendations that take consumer preferences into account. Figure 2.4 shows how priorities differ. Because consumers in Niamey do not necessarily seek to reduce their travel time in a city that has relatively homogeneous neighborhoods compared with Abidjan, which has heavy traffic and is broken up by a lagoon, policy efforts can be directed at the preconsumer trade, especially on improving wholesale market logistics that directly affect product quality and price. In Rabat, where inequalities have increased, ensuring nearby access to quality food in under-privileged neighborhoods may require more interventionist policies. Finally, in Abidjan, where proximity is not an issue because the authorities have imposed retail markets in most neighborhoods, improving consumer transportation is the most important goal. The next section examines how distributors choose where to locate according to these preferences.

Figure 2.4 Consumers' Criteria for Selecting a Location to Purchase Food: Abidjan, Rabat, and Niamey

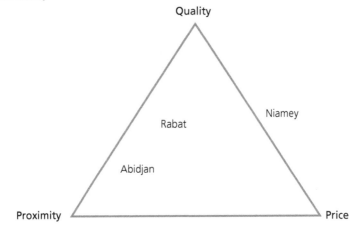

Source: AFD study team.

Food Distributors: Microretailers, Retail Markets, and Supermarkets

Consumers obtain food from an extremely diverse set of retail food distributors that can be classified by their degree of formality. Whether informal micro-retailers or entirely formal supermarkets, the actual progression of consumer food supply options is smoother than illustrated in figure 2.5.[3] Intermediaries are also distinguished by their size and facilities, the type and variety of products offered, and so on.

In general, there is a negative correlation between a country's per capita GDP and its formal share of retail trade (Bachas, Gadenne, and Jensen 2019). An Engel curve of informality explains this correlation. Within a country, it is a function of household income: the highest-income households tend to buy goods from more formal types of stores. For example, in Morocco household income levels drive large behavioral differences, whereas the income effect is almost nonexistent in Niger. The next sections describe the role each of these types of distributors play in food and nutrition security in terms of their ability to satisfy consumer demands for price, quality, variety, and proximity.

Figure 2.5 **Relative Formality of Consumer Food Supply Options**

Source: AFD study team.

Microretailers: Essential in the Poorest Neighborhoods

Street vendor operations are characterized by a low or nonexistent level of capital investment, with little to no equipment and very low stocks of goods (Ananth, Karlan, and Mullainathan 2007; Wilhelm 1997). Nevertheless, the role of (semi-)informal sellers can hardly be underestimated: informal trade is one of the most common jobs in emerging cities. Resnick (2017) indicates that 80–90 percent of milk purchases are made through informal channels, and 70 percent of urban African households regularly purchase from microretailers.

Microretailers also play a major role in ensuring security in the poorest neighborhoods. From a consumer's point of view, microretailers replace transportation infrastructure and offer nearby services—solving the last mile problem—in exchange for lower-priced products but that feature less quality and variety. The effect of informality on affordability is often ambiguous: low stocks force vendors to sell their goods quickly, which may lower prices. Informality allows microretailers to avoid some types of taxes, but it can also put them at risk of hostilities from the authorities or subject them to informal lenders and high interest rates. In general, microretailers charge higher prices because of transport costs and upstream losses. The kind of vendor is also important to take into account. Often, they are women. In fact, a study based on six cases in Sub-Saharan Africa indicates that the majority of microretailers are women—often the only person in the household working (Mitullah 2003). Most microretailers have only a primary school education.

The three cases presented here confirm these findings. In Abidjan, for example, consumer surveys indicate that 83 percent of marketplace customers also buy from microretailers, compared with 26 percent who buy from large and small supermarkets. Large grocery retailers have understood this: some use microretailers to sell to their customers. Importers in Côte d'Ivoire may sell their products to microretailers on credit.

In Niamey, microretailers play a vital role. In the absence of a structured network of retail markets, they link wholesale markets to consumers. For example, whereas the sugarcane wholesaler is located on the periphery, vendors with wheelbarrows full of sugarcane can roam city streets and neighborhoods. In another example, a 2012 fire at Niamey's Petit Marché caused significant losses of goods, facilities, and even cash savings that sellers had stashed in their stalls. It also caused a loss of direct and indirect jobs and broke the chain of solidarity and trust. Meanwhile, Petit Marché businesses resettled in nearby streets. A minority of traders, with encouragement from the national government, relocated to wholesale markets on the urban periphery. This reorganization created difficulties, notably an increase in microretailers and the privatization of public space, which implies that using streets for a commercial space reduces the street's other functions, such as carrying vehicular traffic, thereby creating problems on major roadways.

In Rabat, the number of microretailers has declined as food supply sources have become more complex and numerous. Nevertheless, microretailers remain important, especially in poor neighborhoods, where, according to the census, between 5,000 and 6,000 live. They tend to use the same sources as other resellers, but purchase smaller quantities from the closest urban wholesale markets to reduce their travel distance. Consumers perceive microretailers' products as very low quality. The International Center for Advanced Mediterranean Agronomic Studies indicates that 93 percent of consumers think that street vendor foodstuffs present significant health risks, compared with 10 percent who view souk (neighborhood) products negatively (CIHEAM Agri-Med 2006). The authorities perceive microretailers as an archaic distribution mode, in contrast with modern modes such as supermarkets. In conclusion, microretailers provide an important service as nearby intermediaries. Although their lack of equipment means they can provide only a few products for short periods of time, microretailers remain competitive by reducing the distance consumers must travel for food supplies, particularly in the poorest neighborhoods. However, their institutional fragility vis-à-vis the authorities poses a dilemma for public policy. Microretailers play an essential role, but because of their informal status, they are threatened by authorities. Any intervention strategy should take into account its effects on microretailers.

Retail Markets: Infrastructure and Location in the City

In Abidjan, the national government imposed one central retail market per neighborhood. As noted earlier, the differences between wholesale and retail markets have eroded; several retail markets also have open-air unloading areas. Consumers can choose from about 120 retail markets that have arisen in response to urban development (Poyau 2005). A recent survey counted 165 total markets, a sharp increase since 2005 (graph 2.2). Although public authorities mandate where central markets will be built, as the number of markets multiplies, a dynamic private sector response to rapid urban development is emerging, along with a race for attractive retail spaces.

Graph 2.2 Number of Inhabitants per Neighborhood and Market, Abidjan

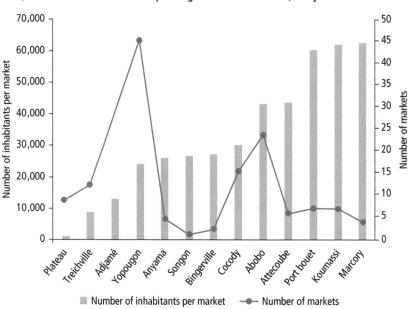

Source: Lançon and Boyer 2019.

The race for the best retail space has also increased inequalities. The number of markets per inhabitant greatly varies by neighborhood (graph 2.2). Neighborhoods with the most shoppers, such as Abobo and Adjamé, have two grands marchés, Abobo Grand Market and the Adjamé Forum, which draw shoppers from across the capital. In map 2.6, findings from consumer surveys show that Adjamé Forum shoppers come from the entire city, especially along its north-south axis. The same is true for the Abobo Grand Market, albeit to a lesser extent. Other market catchment areas are more isolated, in the sense that consumers live near markets and tend to buy only nearby. For example, the Banco 2 Market, which is located in the lower-class Yopougon neighborhood, is much more isolated. Survey respondents live near the market and mostly frequent places in the neighborhood because they value proximity (34 percent) and feel loyalty to the vendors (32 percent). Most central markets, such as the Adjamé Forum, attract customers by offering lower prices, which central markets can do because they are larger, are more competitive, are located near wholesale markets, and can benefit from economies of scale, thereby offering commodity products for 15 percent less on average.

Markets coexist with informal microretailers who buy from open-air unloading areas and sell near households, which reinforces continuity between different types of sales outlets. The more structured a market, the more it will try to strengthen its infrastructure and exclude informal sellers from its perimeter. Thus in Cocody, an affluent neighborhood, the market has tables and a roof but no open-air unloading area nearby, leaving space for clean infrastructure unencumbered by heavy truck traffic. By contrast, in Yopougon, a poorer neighborhood, a cooperative, Coopérative de Distribution de Produits Vivriers de Yopougon (CODIPROVY), manages the market, which, having less access to capital and weaker relations with public authorities, is an open-air unloading area full of trucks and sheds that retails products to less well-off customers.

Niamey has a much less extensive network of local markets. Retailers source products from central markets, whose role varies according to the food distribution chain. A survey of traders revealed that retail markets mostly sell grains, fresh fruit, vegetables, and a few animal products. Complex distribution channels prevent the formation of an equilibrium price. The variations seem stronger than in the more structured case of Abidjan. In addition, the lack of infrastructure leads to frequent cold chain breaks, which probably explains why the local markets do not sell much meat.

Retailers in Rabat may be even more diverse than those in Niamey and Abidjan. As in other cities, informal sellers in Rabat remain, and they are responding to the challenges posed by rapid urbanization. As shown in map 2.7, multiple small informal service providers and intermediaries, such as microretailers, work alongside or inside the institutionalized Bouknadel wholesale market or in the Témara and Salé open-air unloading areas around the city's periphery. Raimundo, Crush, and Pendleton (2016) suggest that the degree of informality negatively correlates with income level, which explains the increased competition between supermarkets in high-income neighborhoods and retailers' search for cheap products for low-income neighborhoods.

Map 2.6 **Shoppers' Places of Residence and Alternative Markets: Adjamé Forum and Banco 2 Market, Abidjan**

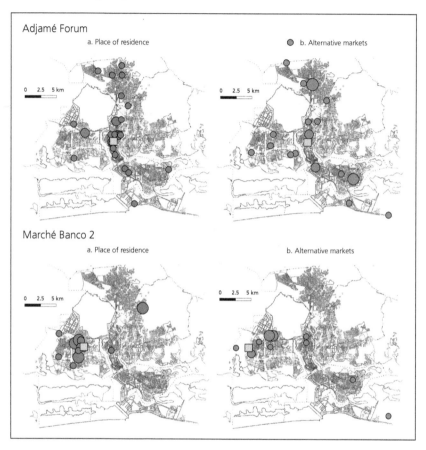

Source: Lançon and Boyer 2019.

Note: The blue circles indicate where shoppers surveyed in each market reside. The green squares indicate the location of the Adjamé Forum and Banco 2 markets. The orange circles indicate the locations of other markets that the surveyed shoppers frequent.

In the *medina*, an old central neighborhood that has somewhat declined economically, trade remains dynamic because of the high density of small, specialized stores, which have surface areas of less than 10 square meters. The basic products are purchased from wholesalers in Salé about twice a week, which makes it possible to partially compensate for low-performance equipment. Nevertheless, the transportation infrastructure in the neighborhood is insufficient.

Map 2.7 **Types of Food Retailers in Rabat's Hay Riad Neighborhood, 2004 and 2016**

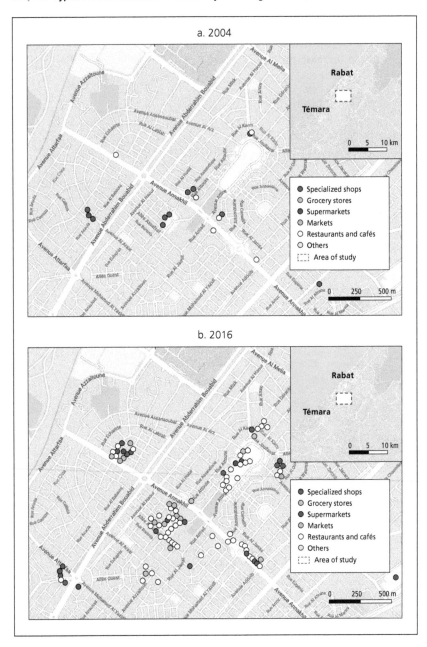

Source: Rousseau and Harroud 2019.

This section has described the diversity of retail markets and their location and infrastructure constraints, illustrating possible avenues for public policy intervention. In particular, it has shown the most obvious inequality between neighborhoods: the inadequate infrastructure in poor neighborhoods, which also tends to increase transportation costs. The last section of this chapter returns to this subject.

Supermarkets and Shopping Centers

The arrival of supermarkets in emerging countries has been described as a "revolution" (Reardon, Timmer, and Minten 2012), driven in part by multinational supermarket chains and in part by domestic entrepreneurs. In emerging countries between 2000 and 2012, the share of household spending at traditional markets fell from 80 percent to 57 percent (Bronnenberg and Ellickson 2015). This decline was mainly concentrated in Eastern Europe and Latin America, where supermarkets account for about 50 percent of retail food sales (Reardon 2012). Often present in secondary and tertiary cities, supermarkets have derived their success from their ability to provide low-cost food, exploit economies of scale, and attract emerging middle-class customers. Atkin, Faber, and Gonzalez-Navarro (2018) conclude that the entry of multinational supermarket chains in Mexico resulted in lower prices for households and gains in affordable food varieties of a magnitude equivalent to a 6 percent increase in household income. This outcome is due in part to the price-lowering effect of supermarket competition on traditional food retailers and sellers. Supermarkets have not penetrated the African continent to as great a degree. Although they are somewhat more present in North and East Africa, they remain marginal in West Africa. Sagaci Research found that in 2015 large and medium-size supermarkets accounted for 10 percent of sales floor space in West Africa, compared with 50 percent in North Africa and 24 percent in East Africa (Sagaci Research 2015). Supermarkets in South Africa lead the way, with 50–60 percent of sales in 2003 through several regional chains such as Shoprite. It is only a question of time when the supermarket revolution will reach Sub-Saharan Africa (ACET 2013).

Supermarket infrastructure differs from that of other types of consumer product distribution facilities. It is more capital-intensive, and it uses refrigeration equipment to offer perishable products. Supermarkets also develop their own supply chains and central purchasing agencies, sometimes buying directly from producers, but more often from intermediaries in wholesale markets. Fully part of the formal economy, supermarkets have employees, which is rarely the case for other food distributors in Africa. Supermarkets are also directly subject to income taxes, whereas other distribution methods are sometimes subject to indirect taxes on transactions. However, because of their capital intensity, supermarkets generate fewer, although better-paid, jobs than do other types of distributors.

Supermarkets locate as close as possible to higher-income consumers, although they have extended their presence to less well-off areas in countries such as Morocco. Therefore, they compete on variety and quality because they use vertical integration or contract farming[4] and thus have more direct control over their value chain than do other traders. Supermarkets also offer lower prices than traditional traders (Rousseau and Harroud 2019, 66), but because they often locate in affluent neighborhoods or on the city periphery (requiring a car to access), they give the proximity advantage to traditional markets and sellers.

In low-income countries such as Niger, supermarkets remain very marginal. Niamey boasts only two supermarkets and some convenience stores. Niamey's supermarkets provide product quality and a pleasant, even ostentatious, buying experience that product prices do not offset. However, the supermarkets have begun to influence some supply chains by sourcing directly from wholesalers and bypassing the lack of a well-defined wholesale marketplace. This situation contrasts with that in Abidjan, where large supermarkets and supermarket chains are expanding—Mieu (2016) estimates they represent 15–20 percent of food sales. Abidjan counts three major supermarket chains, including two major local brands (Lançon and Boyer 2019) that belong to the country's largest private sector companies, Prosuma[5] and Carré d'Or Côte d'Ivoire. Both have annual revenue of several hundred million euros. Prosuma, founded in 1966, had 3,600 employees in 2015. Carré d'Or, founded in 1998, had 6,000 employees in 2015. A French supermarket chain, Carrefour, recently entered the country.

The Côte d'Ivoire supermarket chains use sources that run parallel to traditional distribution infrastructure. For example, within wholesale markets a requirement for quality leads to working with preferred intermediaries. This does not necessarily mean buying imports—most of the chains' fresh tomatoes come from local producers. Prosuma and Carré d'Or, the two largest supermarket chains, purchase from intermediaries who know the retailers' minimum quality criteria, such as large, unbruised fruit, and who can supply large enough lots. Products purchased from wholesalers are sent to each chain's sorting and packing facility to be placed in trays, crates, or other packaging that meets its presentation criteria. Ivorian supermarket chains have also begun to vertically integrate their value chains by forming direct purchase relationships with producer cooperatives, allowing upstream quality control and supplier stability.[6] Furthermore, a new type of food distribution infrastructure—shopping malls— is being built in the affluent or wealthy neighborhoods of Abidjan (Poyau 2005). Intended for the richest shoppers, this type of infrastructure excludes the poorest a little more, possibly reducing the number of retail outlets available to them. This concern may be attenuated by supermarket chains that target poorer neighborhoods, as does Prosuma's Cash King, for example. Nevertheless, discount supermarkets in disadvantaged neighborhoods may compete with the fragile jobs of microretailers.

Supermarkets have been established in Rabat for a longer time, since 1989. Therefore, their effects are easier to discern. As in other countries, legislation allows supermarkets to choose where to locate. Urban planners pose an obstacle, but municipal officials, lured by the tempting contribution to jobs and local revenues, frequently bypass the planners. Pro-supermarket legislation and practices in Morocco have underpinned supermarkets' explosive growth since they first appeared, with 20 stores opening in 2001, and more than 100 in 2010. Supermarkets also appeared in secondary Moroccan cities beginning in 2003. Rabat hosts about 80 different supermarket brands. Map 2.8 shows their locations, mainly in the center of Rabat and on highways along the periphery, where the stores have good connections to transport infrastructure. Because of their locations, the largest supermarkets target well-off customers who have a car (Lagakos 2016). Other supermarkets target middle-class customers, segmenting the market and preferring locations served by public transportation, while competitive and diversification strategies have led the BIM supermarket chain to locate in lower-income neighborhoods.

Map 2.8 **Location of Large and Medium-Size Supermarkets: Rabat, Salé, and Témara, 2016**

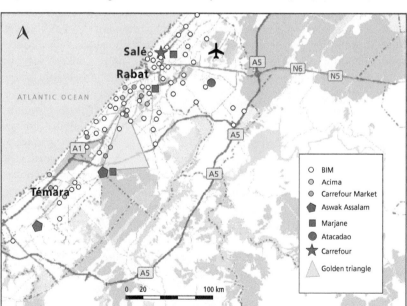

Source: Rousseau and Harroud 2019. Map created by Andrea Mathez and illustrated by Tanika.

In conclusion, retail markets and supermarkets are structured and differentiated by two principal variables: their location and their combination of product quality, price, and variety. They adapt to market conditions and segment urban spaces according to their target consumers. This offers policy makers a number of levers for action in the medium term, such as building or supplying market infrastructure and improving transport conditions. Ultimately, however, consumer preferences determine whether the marketing strategies of supermarket chains will be successful, just as they decide whether the most fragile microretailers will be successful. The next section looks at these preferences.

Food Distribution Infrastructure: Reinforcing Inequalities?

Commercial strategies tend to reinforce existing inequalities by obliging consumers from poorer neighborhoods to spend more of their time shopping or by offering products of dubious hygienic quality. They can even fragment urban spaces, reserving some stores for customers who can access adequate transportation, principally personal cars. However, this does not mean that the concept of urban "food desert" applies in Africa. The concept, which is applied to cities in developed countries, highlights the lack of access that residents of many poor urban neighborhoods in the United States and Europe have to fresh fruits, vegetables, dairy products, and meats (see, for example, Weatherspoon et al. 2013; Wrigley et al. 2002). Because such neighborhoods lack a supermarket, poor residents have no nearby choices other than high-calorie, low-nutrient food. Allcott et al. (2019) recently challenged the food desert concept, showing that the availability of an additional supermarket does not necessarily lead to more purchases of healthy foods.

Applying the urban food desert concept to Africa tends to distract from the central problems: physical accessibility and economic affordability. Formal long chain distribution does not necessarily affect either problem as much as the extent of an informal sector that connects wholesalers and consumers. According to Battersby and Crush (2014), African food insecurity should not be used directly as an argument about the relevance of food deserts. The problem is not the lack of supermarkets in poor neighborhoods, but rather that supermarkets compete with the informal sector and weaken microretailers and other small markets. For example, increasing food insecurity stalks the Sahb El Caïd neighborhood, one of the poorest, in central Salé. Consumers' prioritization of lower cost does not encourage stores to improve product storage conditions, undermining hygiene and overall food quality. In the Hay Karima (Salé) neighborhood, a former shantytown known as a major trading area, businesses are threatened with decline as in Rabat. Transportation plays a role in this decline because easy access to a tram has increased competition from supermarkets. Specialty food stores have also seen their numbers decline, while newer grocery stores fight the competition with updated facilities and offerings. The trend in the wealthiest neighborhoods runs in the opposite direction, with specialty shops increasing their density, taking advantage of supermarket-driven agglomeration effects. For example, the affluent Hay Riad neighborhood in Rabat saw the arrival of specialized stores and restaurants between 2004 and 2016.

Supermarkets, a private sector solution to deficient urban food distribution infrastructure, address only some of the problems. By integrating their logistics operations, they solve the quality problem. But because supermarkets locate in wealthier neighborhoods or those accessible by car, they solve the food security problem only for those who can afford to shop at supermarkets. However, logistical progress appears to be reaching poorer neighborhoods via discount supermarkets, such as King Cash in Abidjan. Looking at South Africa, Battersby and Crush (2014) note that consumers buy different types of goods from traditional retail outlets versus supermarkets, making infrequent trips to supermarkets to purchase basic goods, and more rarely using supermarkets for frequent purchases of vegetables, fruits, and meat. Food choices have certainly decreased in some outlying neighborhoods of Rabat where food insecurity is spreading, such as in Sahb El Caïd, formerly a peripheral slum. Although low incomes are a contributing factor, so are food transport conditions and the relative isolation of the neighborhood. By contrast, Tamesna, a newer suburban neighborhood, has better maintained its food security by supplying itself directly from farmers.

The Role of Public Policies

Transport, Storage, and Processing Infrastructure: Means of Improving Accessibility

Transport as a Key Component of Food Policy

The range of possible policy interventions in physical food supply and distribution infrastructure does not begin or end with markets. Shipping and transport costs strongly affect producer, intermediary, and consumer choices, making transport policy one of the most important levers in urban food infrastructure policy (see AFD 2017 for all levers available to local authorities for food policy actions). Increased investment in roads and public transportation directly affects the accessibility of facilities and therefore the ability of consumers to choose among retail food outlets. It also has indirect effects on territorial development, as described for farming areas at the outset of this chapter. Recent articles provide a better understanding of these effects on a regional scale in India (Donaldson 2018) and on an urban scale (Redding and Turner 2015). For example, in a recent study of the Transmilenio of Bogotá, Tsivanidis (2018) shows that reductions in transportation costs leads to a redistribution of companies and workers, especially the most skilled workers.

These facts and theories are important for food security decisions. Better connecting a market to the rest of the city has upstream effects because producers and other suppliers are able to reduce their shipping costs. It also has downstream effects because consumers have easier access. However, better connections to one market can also have negative effects on other markets, increasing demand, congestion, and the value of nearby land. Therefore, transport infrastructure and market facilities must be considered jointly.

Shipping Costs and Product Perishability

Shipping costs include some wastage costs. Seidou (2012) indicates that, on average, 13.8 percent of village-grown chickens die en route to Niamey's retail markets via public transport because product transport infrastructure is overloaded and there are few storage facilities. Surveys of traders find that the cold chain is not well controlled.[7] For example, it is consistently applied to meat in only one-third of cases, which is particularly worrying for frozen products. Fewer than half of the shippers surveyed had small trucks, and none had a vehicle specifically for meat products. These shortcomings also affect consumer preferences. Shoppers therefore turn to more local products for foods that would require refrigeration and prefer live animals, which cost even more to transport. Another problem tops up this list: Seidou (2012) estimates that retailers receive poultry supplies only two or three times a week, which means that the live chickens stay in cages for several days. Therefore, as with this example and others, improvements in transport infrastructure could reduce consumer costs by reducing wastage. For example, in Rabat improvements in the conditions for shipping tomatoes reduced wastage to an estimated 1 kilogram per case (about 3.5 percent).

The Opportunity: Processing Commercial Products

Processing also reduces transport costs because processed products usually withstand long-distance shipping better than fresh products. When refrigeration is limited, other interventions can help, such as encouraging the local food processing industry to increase product shelf life. Doing so would also create jobs and increase demand for locally grown foodstuffs. Canned goods, often distributed through channels different than those for fresh products, would diversify the product range in stores. Processing is often necessary for meat (such as canning and use in prepared meals) to avoid spoilage of meat kept in the open air.

Food processing requires space, capital investment, and better connections between relevant spaces. Better waste disposal management could also reduce food wastage and increase employment. Storage facilities can serve as well as important food policy levers. Their absence is a major market infrastructure weakness, as noted earlier. A lack of storage facilities makes it impossible to smooth prices throughout the year, worsening both low-availability and high-priced off-season periods between harvests. Graphs 2.3 and 2.4 illustrate that in Niger the price of tomatoes can vary by a factor of five between April and July and by a factor of four for moringa. These economically suboptimal price fluctuations endanger food security. More storage capacity would smooth prices and provide gains to both sellers and consumers.

Identifying Responsibilities for Food Market Location, Construction, Maintenance, and Operation

All three case studies reveal that national or local government intervention plays a central role in configuring market infrastructure. As observed for whole-sale markets, Morocco's national-level decision to require fruits and vegetables to be sold through wholesale markets explains the market structure in Rabat at the local level. Despite considerable informal sector avoidance of the regulation, this decision initially intensified relations between producers and wholesalers and improved price formation. Now, however, it tends to be too rigid to accommodate changing supply and demand dynamics (Rousseau and Harroud 2019). The lack of national and local government regulatory decisions in Niger and Côte d'Ivoire has led to the private sector making most decisions about wholesale and retail market facilities, with the exception of a local government decision in Côte d'Ivoire to impose one retail market in each neighborhood. As a result, each of Abidjan's neighborhoods has a retail market, unlike in Niamey.

How are these decisions made? How are food policies governed? The history of local governance in one in which an overall mission to ensure food security is faced with limited capacity and few tools to do so. In particular, local authorities in Africa, having only recently received skills training and knowledge transfers, do not yet have the staff and financial means to exercise these skills.

Hybrid Public-Private Governance

The governance of urban food systems in general and market infrastructure in particular is complex. Food security can be perceived as a public good, and even a global public good and a Sustainable Development Goal (Clemens and Kremer 2016). Therefore, food security justifies government intervention and possibly funding from external partners. But what form should interventions take, and who should take charge of the interventions? Among different types of market infrastructure, it is easy to move quickly from public goods (transport) through a hybrid good (wholesale markets) to purely private goods (most retail markets). Although governments have long intervened directly in food production, distribution, and prices, such interventions became unpopular in the 1990s. The private sector's purview broadened to include deciding where to locate shops, some markets, and supermarkets and setting prices and contracts, thereby making market infrastructure club goods dependent on members and access rules.

Graph 2.3 Price of 25-Kilogram Box of Tomatoes: Burkina Faso and Niger, April 2015–April 2016

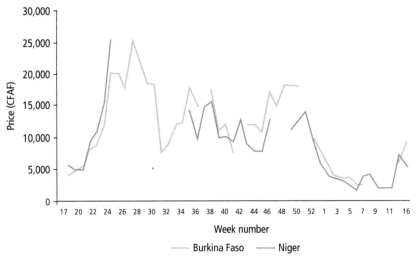

Source: D'Angelo and Brisson 2019.

Graph 2.4 Wholesale Price of 50-Kilogram Bag of Moringa: Déjmadjé and Harobanda (Niamey) Markets, April 2015–April 2016

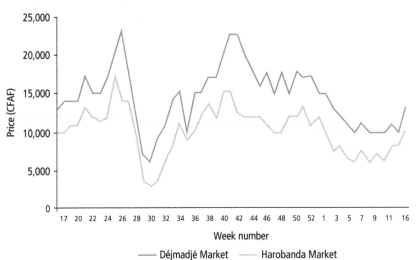

Source: D'Angelo and Brisson 2019.

Markets are also commons, as defined by Elinor Ostrom (1990). She finds that the supply of certain so-called public goods can be provided by community-imposed standards of behavior. The often-informal nature (at least initially) of markets, and the importance of repeated interactions in market transactions— an important value emphasized in consumer and distributor surveys, as noted earlier—means these standards can take hold without government intervention. This hybrid governance explains how and why the interests of private sector actors, community groups such as unions and neighborhood associations, and national and municipal government interventions meet in marketplaces. To be effective, planned government interventions should consult with these three modes of governance, involving national ministries, municipal authorities, producer unions, neighborhood associations, market trader groups, and microretailers. In the three case studies, this apparent institutional complexity overlaps with the equally complex governance of food systems. Although there are significant differences among them, figure 2.6 gives a general outline of these governance levels and types. In this schematic, the Ministry of Agriculture is the principal actor. Together with the Ministry of Health, it covers health safety issues, but otherwise covers farming and all related areas, especially agricultural development, which includes marketing support for farmers. The Ministry of Commerce creates and oversees market regulations and applies standards to wholesale markets. The Ministry of Transport covers road, rail, and (sometimes) maritime infrastructure.

Decentralization has increased municipal authorities' governance of food systems, but it has also added confusion about the division of responsibilities. Although transfers of power have taken place, decentralization sometimes remains mere window dressing. In Côte d'Ivoire, for example, the Ministry of Construction, Sanitation, and Urbanism, in charge of building permits and demolition, directly influences the construction of commercial facilities. Ivorian municipalities are responsible for managing and creating markets, without food supply provision being clearly attributed to them. With levies on local market activities often their major source of revenue, municipalities have little financial capacity and limited resources, which in turn limits their ability to manage new responsibilities and spurs them to delegate some decisions to the private sector. In Sub-Saharan Africa, for example, a weak government capacity for planning and implementing urban food policies helps explain why the main function of markets is to contribute to local finances. In Niger and Côte d'Ivoire, transaction taxes act—or are perceived to act—as a major source of municipal resources (Balineau and Madariaga 2019). Other such cases exist elsewhere in the region.[8] This situation leads to possible revenue capture behaviors in which the goal of maximizing local revenue takes precedence over the goal of developing markets for better food and nutrition security.

Insufficient administrative and technical human resources also pose difficulties in the formulation and implementation of food market policy decisions in West Africa.

Figure 2.6 **The Multilevel Governance of Food Systems**

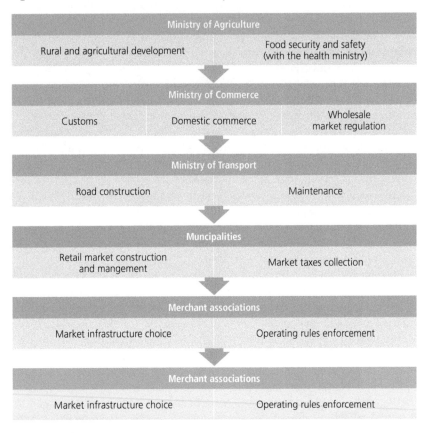

Source: AFD study team.

The lack of resources allocated to understanding market infrastructure dynamics deserves consideration. For example, despite a 2017 Ministry of Commerce initiative to conduct a systematic inventory of the country's marketplaces and open-air unloading areas, Côte d'Ivoire still has no such inventory. Niger has none as well. These knowledge gaps prevent understanding how market infrastructure works and thus identifying problems and effective solutions. The sector's informal nature also makes data acquisition difficult.

In Côte d'Ivoire, the Office d'aide à la commercialisation des produits vivriers (OCPV, or Food Products Marketing Office) and in Niger the Office des Produits Vivriers du Niger (OPVN, or Nigerien Food Products Office), each supervised by its country's Ministry of Commerce, play a special role in the surveying, managing, and promoting of commercial food producers and sellers. In Côte d'Ivoire, the OCPV has formed rural cooperatives and supported business networking, but its sparse resources and the market's complexity make such a mission difficult. In Niger, the OPVN has a broader mission that encompasses the entire food distribution chain, including food aid and offering its own storage and transport capacities to farmers and traders. The OPVN serves as the main tool for preventing the food crises that affect Niger every three years or so. Indeed, recent events have bestowed special importance on food security. A high commissioner to the Nigerien prime minister prepares responses in the event of a crisis, increasing efficiency in a complex administrative context. The OPVN is responsible for food stocks. It sells its stocks to avoid price surges, especially off-season between harvests. Municipalities take care of distributing the food to avoid speculation. The national government's focus on managing food crisis risks leaves it with fewer resources for long-term planning. Moreover, because urban farming continues to be significant in Niamey, the municipality also gives impetus to local agricultural policy, in conjunction with the Ministry of Agriculture.

Important governance functions in all three countries studied rarely explicitly include food distribution issues. National transport infrastructure, so important in structuring the choices of consumers and traders, is the responsibility of the public works ministries. Government engineers often take urban traffic patterns into account, but not necessarily in relation to food distribution issues. The same is true for urban public transportation systems.

Private Sector Food Distributors and the Risk of Conflicts

Driven by the market liberalization in the 1980s, private sector food distributors have gained strength, creating space for local-level sellers unions to organize and choose the locations and facilities they need. For example, municipal food markets in Abidjan are usually created through public-private partnerships (PPPs). Municipalities collect a market tax and a tax for public space use from traders outside markets. Poyau (2005) found that most of the markets in Abidjan were built through PPPs. Because public regulations specify that markets must be built in each district of Abidjan but municipalities lack resources, PPPs allow the private sector to contribute to the erecting of such markets. However, this arrangement reduces the control of public authorities: PPPs often exist outside the urban plan and result from negotiations between municipal officials and private developers. Municipalities' delegation of responsibilities to private institutions also highlights cities' complicated mission to collect a large share of their fiscal resources from food markets. In Morocco, for example, the law requiring fruit and vegetable sellers to use wholesale markets originated in a desire to capture part of the sales value. However, traditional analysis has found PPP contracts to be a suboptimal allocation of risk and cash flow. National governments and international bodies could propose new types of contracts in which municipal authorities could receive more value from their land resources while reducing indirect market transaction taxes, which the consumer ultimately pays.

In Côte d'Ivoire, municipalities have strong links to commercial cooperatives. Municipalities often fund setting up the cooperatives in order to have an interlocutor within the markets. In addition, the Single Act for Cooperative Societies Law recently gave cooperatives a legal framework. These cooperatives manage the markets and market infrastructure, but their lack of means often limits their choices. The line drawn between formal and informal is debatable. In some cases, municipalities recognize markets; in others, cities use a cooperative's informal status to challenge its property rights. Lançon and Boyer (2019) discuss cases in which conflicts with the authorities hampered the development and formalization of two cooperatives. One, in the municipality of Yopougon, owned its land but failed to modernize its structures because it had no administrative relationship with municipal authorities. Another had a conflict with the Adjamé municipality because it would not formalize the cooperative's saleswomen. Cooperatives can also propose ideas. For example, the Federation of Cooperatives began building a wholesale market 30 kilometers from Abidjan with national government support. In all the cases studied, however, the voice of the consumer is little heard, especially in the poorest countries.

Conclusion

This chapter has sought to answer practical and normative questions about how to regulate and optimally set up physical market infrastructure. Geographical and urban economics provide powerful tools to understand the main levers of policy action and their limits—distance still costs too much in Sub-Saharan Africa, including the cost of wasted perishables. Large capital investments are needed, but private and public actors find it difficult to access capital and credit, and often inefficient government regulations do not correct market distortions. As this chapter has sought to clarify, the primary restraint to trading efficiency is not distance but rather a market's economic architecture. Chapter 3 examines this finding further, showing how trust and information, or their absence, can reduce trade efficiency as much as a dilapidated physical market infrastructure can.

Notes

1. The difference between tomatoes and potatoes may seem surprising, However, other centrifugal forces related to globalization have pushed tomato farms, but not potato farms, away from urban areas, as detailed in the following section.
2. These surveys were completed by 312 respondents in Abidjan, 76 in Rabat, and 70 in Niamey. The findings for Rabat and Niamey are not statistically representative.
3. E-commerce adds one level to the distribution chain, although it is virtually nonexistent in Côte d'Ivoire, Morocco, and Niger (World Bank 2019). Nevertheless, e-commerce holds promise. Jumia, an e-commerce site created in Nigeria and active in 15 African countries, was listed on the New York Stock Exchange in April 2019, and became the first African start-up to reach a valuation of more than $1 billion. It includes Jumia Food, a meal delivery platform, and a shopping site. In Kenya, Twyga Foods disrupts the wholesale supply chain, removing the intermediaries between producers and retailers. It recently received financing from the International Finance Corporation.
4. See chapter 3.
5. Ivoirian Supermarket Promotion Company.
6. See chapter 3.
7. Partly because electricity service is unreliable in Sub-Saharan Africa (Blimpo and Cosgrove-Davies 2019).
8. Municipalities perceive markets as a source of revenue for their budget, collecting market fees or an operating fee (AFD 2017). However, this regular cash flow represents only a small share of municipal budgets, ranging from 8 to 28 percent of total municipal resources in several West African cities (Michelon 2012). Recent studies confirm these figures in Madagascar's secondary cities. The low amount can be partially explained by major collection difficulties. In Senegal, for example, market taxes should bring in CFAF 430 million, but collections amount to only CFAF 104 million on average, or barely a quarter of the expected resources (Rouhana, Ranarifidy, and Chomentowski 2014).

References

ACET (African Center for Economic Transformation). 2013. "The Changing Marketplace: The Rise of Supermarkets in West Africa." Accra. http://acetforafrica.org/publications /the-west-africa-trends-newsletter/the-changing-marketplace-the-rise-of-supermarkets -in-west-africa/.

Aderghal, M., S. Lemeilleur, and B. Romagny. 2019. "Contribution des systèmes de distribution alimentaire à la sécurité alimentaire des villes: étude de cas sur l'agglomération de Rabat (Maroc)" [The contribution of food distribution systems to urban food security: Case study of Rabat, Morocco]. Notes techniques, No. 48, Agence française de développement, Paris, February. https://www.afd.fr/fr/nt-48-systeme -alimentaire-qualite-sanitaire-aderghal-lemeilleur-romagny.

AFD (Agence française de développement). 2017. "L'AFD et l'alimentation des villes, quel rôle pour les collectivités locales?" [AFD and urban food: What role can local governments play?]. Paris, September. https://www.afd.fr/fr/lafd-et-l-alimentation -des-villes.

Allcott H., R. Diamond, J.-P. Dubé, J. Handbury, I. Rahkovsky, and M. Schnell. 2019. "Food Deserts and the Causes of Nutritional Inequality." *Quarterly Journal of Economics* 134 (4): 1793–1844.

Allen T. 2017. "Le coût des prix alimentaires élevés en Afrique de l'Ouest" [The cost of high food prices in West Africa]. Notes ouest-africaines, No. 8, Organisation for Economic Co-operation and Development, Paris.

Ananth, B., D. Karlan, and S. Mullainathan. 2007. "Microentrepreneurs and Their Money: Three Anomalies." Working paper, Financial Access Initiative and Innovations for Poverty Action, New York and New Haven, CT.

Andres, L., and P. Lebailly. 2012. "L'approvisionnement agricole de la ville de Niamey: Potentialités et contraintes d'une agriculture de proximité" [The city of Niamey's agricultural supply: Possibilities and constraints of local farming]. Working paper, University of Liège.

Atkin, D., B. Faber, and M. Gonzalez-Navarro. 2018. "Retail Globalization and House- hold Welfare: Evidence from Mexico." *Journal of Political Economy* 126 (1): 1–73.

Bachas, P., L. Gadenne, and A. Jensen. 2019. "Informality, Consumption Taxes and Redistribution." https://pdfs.semanticscholar.org/c587/8872f3b4dd06f245555eff33 99330d2d247e.pdf.

Balineau, G., and N. Madariaga. 2019. "Repenser l'alimentation dans les villes du Sud" [Rethinking food in the urban South]. Question de développement, No. 45, Agence française de développement, Paris, September.

Battersby, J., and J. Crush. 2014. "Africa's Urban Food Deserts." *Urban Forum* 25 (2): 143–51.

Blimpo, M. P., and M. Cosgrove-Davies. 2019. *Electricity Access in Sub-Saharan Africa: Uptake, Reliability, and Complementary Factors for Economic Impact.* Africa Develop- ment Forum. Washington, DC: World Bank. https://openknowledge.worldbank.org /bitstream/handle/10986/31333/9781464813610.pdf.

Boltanski, O., and L. Thévenot. 1991. *De la justification. Les économies de la grandeur* [Justification: Economies of scale]. Paris: Gallimard.

Bronnenberg, B. J., and P. B. Ellickson. 2015. "Adolescence and the Path to Maturity in Global Retail." *Journal of Economic Perspectives* 29 (4): 113–34.

Brunelin, S., and A. Portugal-Perez. 2013. "Food Markets and Barriers to Regional Integration in West Africa." Unpublished document, World Bank, Washington, DC.

Calmette, F. Forthcoming. "Le rôle des marchés dans l'approvisionnement alimentaire des villes: un agenda de recherche basé sur la théorie" [The role of markets in urban food supply: A research agenda based on theory]. Papiers de recherche, Agence française de développement, Paris.

Camara, A. 2016. "Dans quelle mesure la distance est déterminante dans les réseaux d'approvisionnement alimentaire de la ville d'aujourd'hui? Application au cas de la ville d'Abidjan" [How decisive is distance in today's urban food-supply networks? A look at the case of Abidjan]. PhD diss., SupAgro and Cirad, Montpellier.

Chen, K. Z., and K. G. Stamoulis. 2012. "The Changing Nature and Structure of Agri-food Systems in Developing Countries: Beyond the Farm Gate." In *The Transformation of Agri-Food Systems*, edited by E. B. McCullough, P. Pingali, and K. Stamoulis, 167–82. London: Routledge.

CIHEAM Agri-Med. 2006. "Agriculture, pêche, alimentation et développement rural durable dans la région méditerranéenne" [Agriculture, fisheries, food and sustainable rural development in the Mediterranean region]. Annual report, International Center for Advanced Mediterranean Agronomic Studies (CIHEAM), Paris.

Clemens, M. A., and M. Kremer. 2016. "The New Role for the World Bank." *Journal of Economic Perspectives* 30 (1): 53–76.

Cronon, W. 2019. *Chicago, métropole de la nature* [Chicago: Nature's Metropolis], translated by Philippe Blanchard. Paris: Zones Sensibles.

D'Angelo, L., and E. Brisson. 2019. "Systèmes d'approvisionnement et de distribution alimentaires: étude de cas sur la ville de Niamey (Niger)" [Food supply and distribution systems: Case study on the city of Niamey, Niger]. Notes techniques, No. 50, Agence française de développement, Paris, February. https://www.afd.fr/fr/nt-50-marche-alimentation-distribution-groupe8-brisson-emile-geay-dangelo.

Donaldson, D. 2018. "Railroads of the Raj: Estimating the Impact of Transportation Infrastructure." *American Economic Review* 108 (4–5): 899–934.

Fafchamps, M., E. Gabre-Madhin, and B. Minten. 2005. "Increasing Returns and Market Efficiency in Agricultural Trade." *Journal of Development Economics* 78 (2): 406–42. https://ideas.repec.org/a/eee/deveco/v78y2005i2p406-442.html.

Fafchamps, M., and R. V. Hill. 2005. "Selling at the Farm-Gate or Travelling to Market?" *American Journal of Agricultural Economics* 87 (3): 717–34.

FAO (Food and Agriculture Organization of the United Nations). 1996. *Report of the World Food Summit, 13–17 November.* WFS 96/REP, Rome. http://www.fao.org/3/w3548e/w3548e00.htm.

FAO (Food and Agriculture Organization of the United Nations). 2018. "Sustainable Food Systems: Concept and Framework." Rome. http://www.fao.org/3/ca2079en/CA2079EN.pdf.

FAO (Food and Agriculture Organization of the United Nations), WHO (World Health Organization), IFAD (International Fund for Agricultural Development), WFP (World Food Programme), and UNICEF (United Nations Children's Fund). 2018. "The State of Food Security and Nutrition in the World 2018: Building Climate Resilience for Food Security and Nutrition." FAO, Rome. https://www.who.int/nutrition/publications/foodsecurity/state-food-security-nutrition-2018-en.pdf.

Harre, D. M. 2001. "Formes et innovations organisationnelles du grand commerce alimentaire à Abidjan, Côte d'Ivoire" [Organizational forms and innovations of the food trade in Abidjan, Côte d'Ivoire]. *Autrepart* (19): 115–32.

Hotelling, H. 1929. "Stability in Competition." *Economic Journal* 39 (153): 41–57.

IMIST (Institut Marocain de l'Information Scientifique et Technique). 2011. "Le secteur des fruits et légumes au Maroc: état des lieux et perspectives" [The fruit and vegetable sector in Morocco: state of play and prospects]. *Bulletin d'information technologique—industrie agroalimentaire*, No. 20, IMIST, Rabat, Morocco.

Koffie-Bikpo, C. Y., and A. A. Adaye. 2014. "Agriculture commerciale à Abidjan: le cas des cultures maraîchères" [Commercial agriculture in Abidjan: The case of market gardening] *Pour* (224): 141–49.

Krugman, P. 1980. "Scale Economies, Product Differentiation, and the Pattern of Trade." *American Economic Review* 70 (5): 950–59.

Lagakos, D. 2016. "Explaining Cross-Country Productivity Differences in Retail Trade." *Journal of Political Economy* 124 (2): 579–620.

Lançon, F., and A. Boyer. 2019. "Contribution des systèmes de distribution alimentaire à la sécurité alimentaire des villes: étude de cas sur l'agglomération d'Abidjan (Côte d'Ivoire)" [The contribution of food distribution systems to urban food security: Case study of Abidjan, Côte d'Ivoire]. Notes techniques, No. 49, Agence française de développement, Paris, February. https://www.afd.fr/fr/nt-49-systeme-alimentaire-urbanisation-abidjan-lancon-boyer.

Lemeilleur, S., M. Aderghal, O. Jenani, A. Binane, M. Berja, Y. Medaoui, and P. Moustier. 2019. "La distance est-elle toujours importante pour organiser l'approvisionnement alimentaire urbain? Le cas de l'agglomération de Rabat" [Is distance always important for urban food supply production? The case of Greater Rabat]. Papiers de recherche, No. 91, Agence française de développement, Paris. https://www.afd.fr/fr/la-distance-est-elle-toujours-importante-pour-organiser-lapprovisionnement-alimentaire-urbain-le-cas-de-lagglomeration-de-rabat.

Mahyao, A. G. 2008. "Étude de l'efficacité du système d'approvisionnement et de distribution des ignames précoces kponan à travers le circuit Bouna-Bondoukou-Abidjan en Côte d'Ivoire" [Study of the efficiency of the supply and distribution system for early Kponan yams through the Bouna-Bondoukou-Abidjan circuit in Côte d'Ivoire]. Thesis UFR SEG, University of Cocody, Abidjan.

Maire, B., and F. Delpeuch. 2004. "La transition nutritionnelle, l'alimentation et les villes dans les pays en développement" [The nutritional transition, food and cities in developing countries]. *Cahiers Agricultures* 13 (1): 23–30.

Michelon, B. 2012. "Planification urbaine et usages des quartiers précaires en Afrique. Études de cas à Douala et à Kigali" [Urban planning and precarious neighborhood uses in Africa: Case studies in Douala and Kigali]. Thesis No. 5195, École Polytechnique Fédérale de Lausanne.

Mieu, B. 2016. "Côte d'Ivoire: Abou Kassam, un discret patron qui essaime" [Côte d'Ivoire: Abou Kassam, a discreet boss who expands]. *JeuneAfrique.com*. http://www.jeuneafrique.com/mag/289443/economie/cote-divoire-abou-kassam-discret-patron-essaime/.

Mitullah, W. V. 2003. "Street Vending in African Cities: A Synthesis of Empirical Findings from Kenya, Cote D'Ivoire, Ghana, Zimbabwe, Uganda, and South Africa." World Development Report Background Papers, No. 2005, World Bank, Washington, DC.

Ostrom, E. 1990. *Governing the Commons: The Evolution of Institutions for Collective Action.* Cambridge, U.K.: Cambridge University Press.

Oura, R. K. 2012. "Extension urbaine et protection naturelle: la difficile expérience d'Abidjan" [Urban extension and natural protection: Abidjan's difficult experience]. *VertigO—la revue électronique en sciences de l'environnement* 12 (2). https://vertigo.revues.org/12966.

Poyau, A. 2005. "Les récentes mutations des marchés urbains dans la capitale économique ivoirienne" [Recent changes to urban markets in the Ivorian economic capital]. *Espace, Populations, Sociétés* 1: 111–26.

Raimundo, I., J. Crush, and W. Pendleton. 2016. "Food Insecurity, Poverty and Informality." In *Rapid Urbanisation, Urban Food Deserts and Food Security in Africa*, edited by J. Crush and J. Battersby, 71–83. Cham, Switzerland: Springer.

Rao, C. H. H. 2000. "Declining Demand for Foodgrains in Rural India: Causes and Implications." *Economic and Political Weekly* 35 (4): 201–06.

Reardon, T. 2012. "The Global Rise and Impact of Supermarkets: An International Perspective." Proceedings of Crawford Fund 17th Annual Parliamentary Conference, The Supermarket Revolution in Food: Good, Bad or Ugly for the World's Farmers, Consumers and Retailers? August 14–16, 2011, Crawford Fund, Canberra, Australia.

Reardon, T., C. P. Timmer, and B. Minten. 2012. "Supermarket Revolution in Asia and Emerging Development Strategies to Include Small Farmers." *Proceedings of the National Academy of Sciences* 109 (31): 12332–37.

Redding, S. J., and M. A. Turner. 2015. "Transportation Costs and the Spatial Organization of Economic Activity." In *Handbook of Regional and Urban Economics*, Vol. 5, edited by G. Duranton, J. Vernon Henderson, and W. C. Strange, 1339–98. Amsterdam: Elsevier.

Resnick, D. 2017. "Governance: Informal Food Markets in Africa's Cities." In 2017 *Global Food Policy* Report, 50–57. International Food Policy Research Institute, Washington, DC.

Rouhana, S., D. N. Ranarifidy, and V. Chomentowski. 2014. "Stratégie globale d'amélioration des recettes de la Ville de Dakar" [Comprehensive revenue improvement strategy for the City of Dakar]. Public-Private Infrastructure Advisory Facility, Washington, DC. https://ppiaf.org/documents/3164/download.

Rousseau, M., A. Boyet, and T. Harroud. 2019. "Le makhzen et le marché de gros: la politique d'approvisionnement des villes marocaines entre contrôle social and néolibéralisme" [The governing elite and the wholesale market: The supply policy of Moroccan cities straddles social control and neoliberalism]. Papiers de recherche, No. 92, Agence française de développement, Paris. https://www.afd.fr/fr/le-makhzen-et-le-marche-de-gros-la-politique-dapprovisionnement-des-villes-marocaines-entre-controle-social-et-neoliberalisme.

Rousseau, M., and T. Harroud. 2019. "Mutation de la gouvernance des systèmes alimentaires urbains: le cas de l'agglomération de Rabat-Salé" [Changes in urban food system governance: The case of Rabat-Salé], Notes techniques, No. 47, Agence française de développement, Paris, February. https://www.afd.fr/fr/nt-47-systeme-alimentaire-rabat-rousseau-harroud.

Sagaci Research. 2015. "Shopping Malls in Africa." Sagaci Research, Paris. https://www.sagaciresearch.com/product/shopping-malls-across-africa-2015-full-pdf-report/.

Scott, J. C. 2019. *Homo domesticus: une histoire profonde des premiers États* [Homo domesticus: A deep history of the first states]. Paris: La Découverte.

Seidou, A. 2012. "Analyse de l'approvisionnement de la ville de Niamey (Niger) en volailles de basse-cour" [An analysis of backyard poultry supply to Niamey, Niger]. Master's thesis, University Cheick Anta Diop, Dakar.

Tollens, E. 1997. "Wholesale Markets in African Cities. Diagnosis, Role, Advantages and Elements for Further Study and Development." Food Supply and Distribution to Cities in French-Speaking Africa—Food into Cities Collection, AC/05-97, Food and Agriculture Organization of the United Nations and University de Louvain, Rome. http://www.fao.org/3/a-ab790e.pdf.

Tschirley, D., M. Ayieko, M. Hichaambwa, J. Goeb, and W. Loescher. 2010. "Modernizing Africa's Fresh Produce Supply Chains without Rapid Supermarket Takeover: Towards a Definition of Research and Investment Priorities." MSU International Development Working Paper, No. 106, Michigan State University, East Lansing.

Tsivanidis, N. 2018. "The Aggregate and Distributional Effects of Urban Transit Infrastructure: Evidence from Bogotá's Trans Milenio." Working paper, Department of Economics, Dartmouth College, Hanover, NH.

Valette, E., and P. Philifert. 2014. "L'agriculture urbaine: un impensé des politiques publiques marocaines?" [Urban agriculture: An unimaginable public policy in Morocco?] *Géocarrefour* 89 (1-2): 75–83.

Valyans Consulting. 2010. "Étude relative à l'élaboration d'un schéma national d'orientation des marchés de gros de fruits et légumes du Maroc—phase 5: lancement du marché pilote de Rabat, concept et modèle cible" [Study about the development of a national orientation scheme for wholesale fruit and vegetable markets in Morocco. Phase 5: launch of a pilot market in Rabat, concept, and target model]. Unpublished internal document, Valyans Consulting, Paris.

Von Thünen, J. H. 1826. *Der isolierte Staat in Beziehung auf Landwirtschaft und Nationalökonomie.* Hamburg: Perthes. Translation: 1966. The Isolated State. Oxford, U.K.: Pergamon Press.

Weatherspoon, D., J. Oehmke, A. Dembele, M. Coleman, T. Satimanon, and L. Weatherspoon. 2013. "Price and Expenditure Elasticities for Fresh Fruits in an Urban Food Desert." *Urban Studies* 50 (1): 88–106.

Whelan, A., N. Wrigley, D. Warm, and E. Cannings. 2002. "Life in a 'Food Desert.'" *Urban Studies* 39 (11): 2083–100.

Wilhelm, L. 1997. "Transport et approvisionnement intermarchés dans les villes en Afrique: des services méconnus aux usagers, commerçants et consommateurs" [Intermarket transport and supply in cities in Africa: Little-known services to users, traders and consumers]. FAO-ISRA Seminar: Approvisionnement et distribution alimentaires dans les villes africaines francophones, Dakar, Senegal, April 14–17, Food and Agriculture Organization of the United Nations, Rome.

World Bank. 2010. Global Consumption Database. http://datatopics.worldbank.org/consumption/.

World Bank. 2019. *Future of Food: Harnessing Digital Technologies to Improve Food System Outcomes.* Washington, DC: World Bank. https://openknowledge.worldbank.org/handle/10986/31565.

Wrigley, N., D. Warm, B. Margetts, and A. Whelan. 2002. "Assessing the Impact of Improved Retail Access on Diet in a 'Food Desert': A Preliminary Report." *Urban Studies* 39 (11): 2061–82.

Chapter 3

New Private Sector and Government Institutions: Facilitating Market Matching in Abidjan, Rabat, and Niamey

Virtually every commercial transaction has within itself an element of trust, certainly any transaction conducted over a period of time. It can be plausibly argued that much of the economic backwardness in the world can be explained by the lack of mutual confidence.

—Kenneth Joseph Arrow, 1972

This volume has described how various types of physical market infrastructure help to match physical supply and demand through marketplaces, roads, storage facilities, retail distributors, and so forth. Chapter 2 looked at how the various types function and the problems they encounter. However, physical infrastructure on its own is insufficient to match supply and demand. Other important elements are price and quality information, credit, and trust in institutions and contracts. This chapter focuses on nonphysical market infrastructure, or what is called here the institutional market infrastructure or market institutions. Market institutions include all private sector and public sector arrangements that create an environment conducive to trade at all stages of food production and distribution, including so-called soft market infrastructure such as price information systems, contractual arrangements, quality standards, and credit markets.

Context and Problem Identification

Trade's Fundamental Problem in Côte d'Ivoire, Morocco, and Niger

Greif (2000) precisely describes the fundamental problem affecting trade by first questioning the barriers to trade and then identifying the conditions necessary for trade. For example, he states that "a lender will not lend without assurances that the borrower will not invest the money in a doomed project or disappear with the funds; an investor will invest only if he is guaranteed that the government will not subsequently expropriate his assets" (Grief 2000, 251). Similarly, for food supply and distribution, even if there are working roads, consumers will not travel to buy food if they think it is of poor quality. Likewise, wholesalers will not travel if they do not know the prices. They must be confident they will be able to sell their stock and achieve a sufficient profit.

Trade's fundamental problem emerges in situations in which interactions are sequential, and when Party 1 initiates a cooperative trade, Party 2 has an incentive to deviate unilaterally and behave in an uncooperative manner. In anticipation of such a possibility, Party 1 will prefer to not initiate any cooperative trade. According to Greif (2000), "The trade sequence exposes the fundamental problem of trade: an individual will only seek to establish an objectively profitable trading relationship if his counterpart can pre-guarantee that he will fulfill his obligations" (p. 254). When a consumer buys food, its quality will not be revealed until it is cooked or consumed. Therefore, a consumer will decide to buy food only if the seller can convince the consumer of the food's quality during their interaction and before the trade transaction. The problem of quality also involves basic, essential product attributes, including flavor and vertical differentiation. Thus distributors buy from producers they trust, even if only about product weight. Abate et al. (2018) have shown that simply equipping wheat producers in Ethiopia with functioning scales had a positive effect on sales volumes and prices (see Auriol, Balineau, and Bonneton, forthcoming, for a review of quality information asymmetry mechanisms and effects). Thus, "for individuals to enter into a mutually beneficial cooperative trading relationship they must recognize their mutual interest and promise to honor their contractual obligations" (Greif 2000).

In contrast to the medieval merchant societies that Greif studies, what he calls "modern" societies developed institutions that guaranteed the performance of contractual obligations and created conditions favorable for trading relationships. According to Greif (2000), such institutions were able to solve the fundamental problem of trade by ensuring that all contractual obligations were met. For example, a textile producer undertakes to supply a clothing manufacturer with a certain quality of cotton fabric of a particular length and specific color. However, if the shipment received by the manufacturer does not match the order, the manufacturer may return it and receive compensation for the defects. Only high-income countries have this type of legal mechanism—one that guarantees the execution of written contracts. In low-income countries, such mechanisms either do not exist or are very costly to enforce, and so engaging in trade is perceived as riskier because it becomes more expensive if problems arise (see Auriol, Balineau, and Bonneton, forthcoming, and graph 3.1).

Graph 3.1 **Correlation between GDP and Cost of Enforcing Contracts**

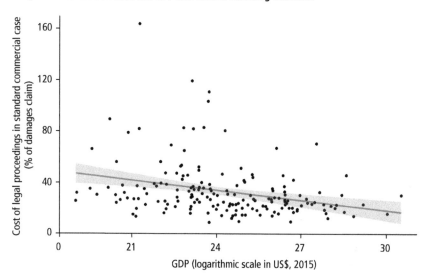

Source: Auriol, Balineau, and Bonneton, forthcoming.

Côte d'Ivoire, Morocco, and Niger do not have credible universal contract enforcement mechanisms or easily accessible market information. And they do have especially low levels of interpersonal trust. This environment creates country-specific problems for their food supply and distribution systems. However, they do have institutions, that although different from those found in high-income countries, make trade possible. This chapter describes the private sector arrangements and public sector interventions that make up these institutions or that foster trusting relationships, thereby helping to solve trade's fundamental problem in Côte d'Ivoire, Morocco, and Niger.

The Role of Contract Enforcement Mechanisms
Mechanisms that enforce contracts and the costs of acquiring information about traded products are central to the issue of trade. As Startz (2018) notes, economic and econometric models that seek to account for trade intensity

between different locations[1] often include an indicator for a common language between localities that captures a certain facility for accessing price information, as well as an indicator for the contractual environment, such as the quality of legal institutions. In the absence of contract enforcement mechanisms, contractual relationships between two trading parties can be described as a repeated game of moral hazard (Startz 2018). The resolution of this model finds that repeated interactions create an incentive for cooperative behavior. The principle is as follows: the buyer, who initiates the transaction and pays before having received the goods, is subject to a price higher than the marginal cost. Therefore, it is more profitable for the seller, in the context of repeated interactions, to not seek the one-off profit generated by uncooperative behavior, such as not delivering the goods, because the discounted sum of current and future profits (including marginal cost and surplus) is greater than the immediate benefit of uncooperative behavior. Startz (2018) shows that intermediary buyers suffer from the absence of effective contract enforcement mechanisms. They gain less profit than in an ideal world in which contracts would be honored even without repeated interactions. In the absence of contract enforcement institutions, buyer size is also larger on average because the smallest buyers cannot overcome the barriers to entry created by these contracting frictions.

The Rule of Law Index of the World Bank (2017a) tracks the absence of contract enforcement mechanisms. It reflects perceptions of the extent to which agents have confidence in and abide by the rules of society, and in particular the quality of contract enforcement, property rights, the police and the courts, as well as the likelihood of crime and violence. The index's estimates are made by synthesizing and standardizing various data sources that describe these components. The index values for Côte d'Ivoire, Morocco, and Niger, as well as those for other major regions, appear in graph 3.2. It reveals that the three countries perform below the world average but better than their Sub-Saharan Africa region.

The Institutional Profiles Database of the Centre d'études prospectives et d'informations internationales (CEPII, or Center for International Outlook Studies and Information) breaks down the Rule of Law Index by sector to create a Security of Contracts and Transactions Index. This component of the Rule of Law Index highlights the significance of the fundamental problem affecting trade and the extent to which institutions can solve it. Graph 3.3 shows that the security of transactions and contracts appears less assured in Côte d'Ivoire, Morocco, and Niger than in the rest of the world, particularly in the goods and services market, the most relevant for studying food distribution systems. The lower level of security remains generally true for labor markets and capital markets, although Morocco provides an exception. For transactions and contracts that fall under the purview of public institutions or civil society, such as property rights, private contracts, commercial justice, bankruptcy law, and state-led contract termination, Morocco and Niger perform less well on security than do other countries on average, whereas Côte d'Ivoire ranks closer.

Thus it appears that the institutional context does not facilitate resolving the fundamental problem of trade in Côte d'Ivoire, Morocco, and Niger. The next section considers the level of interpersonal trust, which could help facilitate trade. However, while discussed separately, these two components—institutions and trust—may influence each other because an effective system for securing trade undoubtedly fosters a more trusting population.

Graph 3.2 Rule of Law Index: Côte d'Ivoire, Morocco, Niger, Other Regions, and World

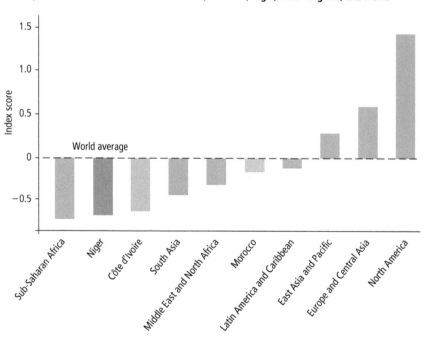

Source: AFD study team, based on Tefft et al. (2017); World Bank (2017a).

Graph 3.3 **Security of Contracts and Transactions Index by Sector: Côte d'Ivoire, Morocco, Niger, and Rest of World**

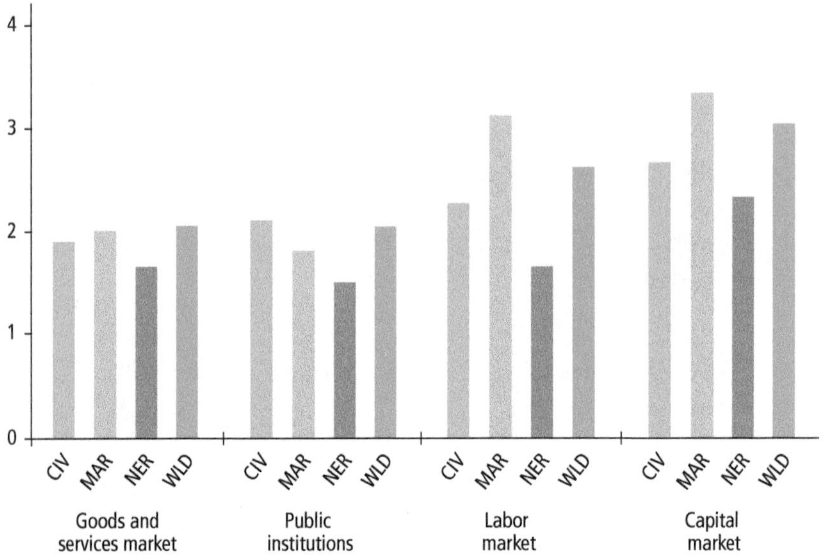

Source: CEPII 2016.

Note: CIV = Côte d'Ivoire; MAR = Morocco; NER = Niger; WLD = rest of world.

The Role of Trust

The economics and social sciences literature have highlighted the existence of cooperation in the absence of contractual obligations to ensure it. Cooperative behavior is often observed in experiments in which anonymous participants play games that are not repeated (Cahuc and Algan 2014)—a behavior observed in individuals from very diverse societies (Bowles et al. 2005; Bowles and Gintis 2007; Fehr 2009). Cahuc and Algan (2014) point to the role of trust in solving trade's fundamental problem—a component particularly difficult to grasp in economics. Modeling trust in the economy involves taking the psychological cost of noncooperation into account. If Party 1 trusts that Party 2 will not deviate because of this psychological cost, Party 1 may choose not to deviate. The economic models deployed by Cahuc and Algan (2014) reveal that the percentage of the population individuals believe is trustworthy affects these individuals' trade intensity with others. The larger this percentage, the higher will be the gains expected by an individual who wants to cooperate and therefore the more he or she will be inclined to initiate an exchange. In other words, in the absence of contract enforcement mechanisms or interpersonal trust, trading is not as intense as it could be—see, for example, Berg, Dickhaut, and McCabe (1995) for empirical validation.

Trust levels in Côte d'Ivoire, Morocco, and Niger fundamentally contribute to reducing friction in food distribution systems. However, these levels are not easy to quantify. The World Values Survey interviews representative samples of people from more than 100 countries, asking if interviewees agree that "most people can be trusted" (Inglehart et al. 2014).[2] Of the three countries studied here, the last survey wave (2010–13) includes only Morocco because all countries are not interviewed in every wave. Despite that, the survey reflects trust levels in 60 countries, including five other Sub-Saharan African countries. Graph 3.4 shows that trust levels are especially low in Morocco and in most Sub-Saharan Africa countries. This result is fairly consistent with the well-established relationship between trust levels and per capita income levels: the higher the per capita income, the higher are the interpersonal trust levels (Knack and Keefer 1997).

Graph 3.4 **Trust Levels: Morocco, Other Countries, and World, 2013**

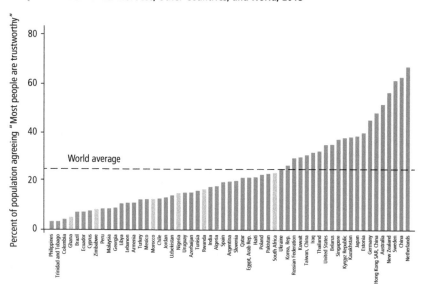

Source: AFD study team, based on Inglehart et al. (2014).

How does this lack of contract enforcement mechanisms or interpersonal trust affect food distribution systems in Côte d'Ivoire, Morocco, and Niger? In the absence of contracts or trust that ensure a transaction's dimensions, specifications, and execution, the buyer must try to obtain guarantees for the price, quality, and other characteristics of a product in order to receive a refund or other compensation if one or more characteristics are not met upon product delivery. This environment amplifies another barrier to trade—difficulty accessing market information, particularly a product's price–quality ratio. A buyer with effective contract enforcement mechanisms could rely on contracts to guarantee product quality even if the buyer failed to investigate a product's quality before purchasing it. Likewise, if trust were high, a buyer could simply rely on the seller's word to assess product quality. However, defective contract enforcement mechanisms and a fairly low level of interpersonal trust make it absolutely necessary for a buyer to obtain product information to guide purchase decisions.

Three Structural Difficulties in Solving Trade's Fundamental Problem

Scarce, Expensive, and Dispersed Market Information

As noted in chapter 2, a buyer's ability to make choices is fundamental to the proper operation of market infrastructure. According to Calmette (forthcoming), a consumer's ability to choose from among sellers located in several places, or among several suppliers, allows markets to function optimally and goods to be allocated appropriately. If a consumer realizes that a product is sold for price p, but that by bearing the transport cost c the same product can be obtained for a price lower than $p - c$, the consumer will bear cost c. However, this only works if the consumer has this price information. If such price information is available to the consumer, the resulting law of one price applies. It holds that the difference in price between the same good sold on two markets must not exceed the cost of transport between their two locations. This result depends on agents who take advantage of arbitrage opportunities. If the price difference is greater than the transport costs, agents buy the good from the market where the price is the lowest and resell the good on the other market.

However, information is often costly to acquire, or it is incomplete (Stigler 1961). As a result, a poor allocation of goods to various markets remains prevalent in West Africa (Brunelin and Portugal-Perez 2013) and in many low-income countries (Jensen 2007). The lack of information precludes efficient distribution systems. It also prevents some trade from occurring and certain suppliers from setting up shop. Thus traders and consumers in some regions remain poorly served or must pay exorbitant prices.

It is not easy to undertake a detailed study of price information accessibility in Côte d'Ivoire, Morocco, and Niger. However, in Niger a market information system (MIS) does provide resale prices on various markets, which should facilitate agents' arbitrage decisions. Araujo, Araujo-Bonjean, and Brunelin (2012) apply a causality test to various markets' price series using a methodology developed by Gupta and Mueller (1982) and adopted by Fackler and Goodwin (2001). The test highlights the nonintegration of many Nigerien markets. The distance between markets represents an obstacle to good price decision-making because a potential buyer has poor information about the products available in various places, and the cost of acquiring such information is too high.

Difficulties in Contracting

The cost of searching for information is linked to the cost of contracting. The lack of an institution to facilitate agreement on product trade terms exacerbates the difficulties of trading inherent in the cost of acquiring information about product characteristics. The absence of quality standards makes a contractual definition of quality harder to articulate. Conversely, the cost of contracting makes quality standards less useful, particularly during the initial upstream food distribution phases. Trade agreements between producers and wholesalers or between wholesalers and retailers are based on oral contracts and subjective quality assessments. Côte d'Ivoire, Morocco, and Niger have quality standard systems that are underdeveloped compared with those of the rest of the world. In addition, costly access to information on quality slows down their trade development as does the lack of standardized quality information. Graph 3.5 presents indicators for the Security of Contracts and Transactions Index for the goods and services markets. Product distribution phases appear to be hindered primarily by the lack of standardized information about the quality of goods and services.

In making buying decisions, consumers and sellers look at prices, with quality on the other side of the coin. Buyers and sellers alike must agree on a price for a certain level of quality. A lack of information about quality can prevent a buyer from making a decision. It can also hinder signing a contract and ultimately affect the market's quality level. In particular, sellers find it difficult to signal quality if there are no quality standards. If sellers cannot influence buyers' perceptions of product quality, they will find it difficult to sell good-quality products at a fair price. Buyers who cannot discern a product's higher quality level will not pay a price higher than the average price of such goods. Thus the lack of quality standards pushes sellers of good-quality products to withdraw from the market. It also prompts buyers to no longer buy at a market if it offers only low-quality goods (Akerlof 1970).

Graph 3.5 shows that Côte d'Ivoire, Morocco, and Niger have lower standards of information on the quality of goods and services than do other countries. One need only look at a chicken market in Morocco to see the direct consequences of lower-quality information standards, illustrating a mechanism conceptualized by Akerlof (1970). Consumers are accustomed to buying only live chickens in the absence of quality signals for chicken parts sold at the market. A market for already-slaughtered chicken therefore cannot exist because of a lack of information about the quality of the chicken parts on offer.

Graph 3.5 **Security of Contracts and Transactions Index in Markets for Goods and Services: Côte d'Ivoire, Morocco, Niger, and Rest of World**

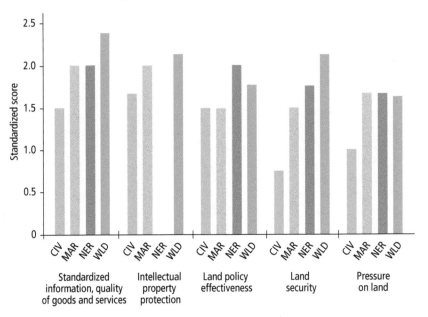

Source: AFD study team, based on CEPII (2016).
Note: Indicator scores are normalized between 0 and 4. A score of 4 indicates a high level of standardized information about goods and services quality, intellectual property protection, land policy effectiveness, land security, and pressure on land. A score of 4 for pressure on land indicates abundant land availability. CIV = Côte d'Ivoire, MAR = Morocco, NER = Niger, WLD = rest of world.

Consumer choice appears to be guided by a perception of quality. However, various conventions affect this perception (Boltanski and Tévenot 1991). Each con-vention uses different instruments to identify quality. Consumers who refer to their beliefs in assessing product quality behave according to an *inspiration* convention. When consumers rely on the trust they place in a seller based on repeated interactions, the domestic convention applies. When consumers use a non-objective external opinion, they behave according to the *opinion* convention. The *industrial* convention is based on a scientifically established system of standards and quality. Thus traditional food distribution systems are often based on the domestic convention (Sylvander 1997). When it dominates, a market can establish itself despite a lack of product quality standards. The industrial convention requires objective, standardized quality standards to guide consumer choice. Because supermarkets are based on the industrial convention, a lack of quality standards can hamper their development.

Another obstacle to contracting is simply the cost of enforcing contracts. The World Bank's (2019) Ease of Doing Business Index is a composite index that aggregates several business climate indicators. One of its components combines attorneys' fees, court fees, and enforcement fees, thereby quantifying the cost of enforcing contracts. These costs, expressed as a percentage of the amount claimed in a dispute, are extremely high in Côte d'Ivoire (41.3 percent) and Niger (52.6 percent), while in Morocco (26.5 percent) they remain higher than the average for high-income Organisation for Economic Co-operation and Development (OECD) countries (21.2 percent). Thus the relatively high cost of enforcing contracts in the three countries makes objective and standardized quality standards less useful for intertrader trade; the expense of setting and meeting norms would inflate the contracting costs, which are already costly to enforce. In addition, contracts exacerbate the trading difficulties generated by the lack of quality standards. High financial costs further restrict contract enforcement mechanisms.

Difficulties in Accessing Credit

Access to credit is essential for an efficient food system because it facilitates farming, expands wholesale enterprises, and creates retail businesses. An efficient credit market, unlike an inefficient one, helps farmers farm, as it does for any entrepreneurial project. Numerous studies have shown that credit market failures constrain farmers' adoption of new agricultural technologies (see Dethier and Effenberger 2011). Credit allows farmers to move capital between two periods, from an initial investment at planting time to harvest time, when sales generate wealth that would not occur in the absence of that initial investment (Casaburi and Willis 2018). Credit therefore smooths wealth levels over time in anticipation of profitable entrepreneurial success by financing the initial investment needed for an entrepreneurial project. Wholesale businesses also require substantial initial capital investments to cover equipment costs and the first inventory purchases. Resale profits amortize the initial investment. However, if entrepreneurs do not have their own funding, even if their business would be profitable, wholesale trading is impossible without access to credit.

Barriers to credit creates barriers to entry for some wholesalers, hampering development of the wholesale trade activity essential to food systems. Retail businesses also often need to acquire sales and storage spaces at a significant fixed cost. As with wholesale businesses, some profitable retail activities will not find funding in the absence of a functioning credit market. Barriers to credit access also present obstacles to food distribution activities.

Graph 3.6 **Credit Use: Côte d'Ivoire, Morocco, Niger, and World, 2017**

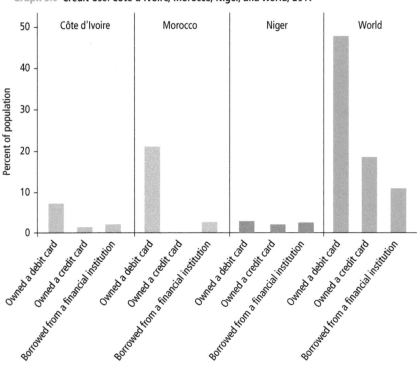

Source: AFD study team, based on Tefft et al. (2017); World Bank (2017b).

Note: Graph shows the percentage of the population ages 15 and up who held a debit card, credit card, or bank loan in 2017.

Developing the financial sector often facilitates access to credit. The Global Financial Inclusion Database of the World Bank (2017b) pinpoints the level of credit market development (see graph 3.6). It depicts the percentage of the population in Côte d'Ivoire, Morocco, and Niger that held a debit card, credit card, or a bank loan in 2017. Access to credit cards appears particularly limited because less than 3 percent of the population over the age of 15 has one, compared with the unweighted world average of nearly 20 percent. The percentage of the population that borrowed money from a bank in the previous year is almost three times lower than the world average of over 10 percent.

The Global Financial Inclusion Database highlights the low level of credit supply and lists the reasons populations do not use financial institutions (graph 3.7). Nearly 20 percent of Nigeriens and Ivorians who do not have a bank account say they lack information about banks or banks are too far away or too expensive (graph 3.7). In Côte d'Ivoire, Morocco, and Niger, poverty levels and

Graph 3.7 Reasons for Level of Access to Financial Services: Côte d'Ivoire, Morocco, and Niger, 2017

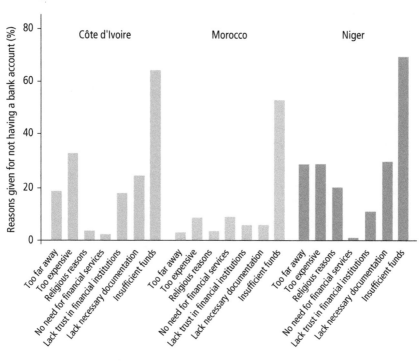

Source: AFD study team, based on Tefft et al. (2017); World Bank (2017b).
Note: Variables are for unbanked population ages 15 years and up.

financial services costs are put forward to justify banks' low market penetration rates. More than half of the unbanked individuals in these countries declare they do not have enough money to open a bank account, which suggests that banks do not offer services suited to this market.[3] As a result, these three countries have particularly low levels of credit use and financial services access. The existing bank savings and credit offerings seem particularly ill-suited to local needs, possibly hindering the development of efficient food production and distribution systems. The following section presents private sector arrangements that have developed in response to the three problems just described: lack of information, absence of quality standards, and lack of credit access.

Developing Private Sector Arrangements to Facilitate Food Supply and Distribution

In this institutional context, private sector arrangements have developed to resolve trade's fundamental problem in the food distribution sector. This is not unique to Côte d'Ivoire, Morocco, Niger, or the sector. Dixit (2004) emphasizes the importance of private sector and nonlegal arrangements in very diverse contexts.[4] Discussing trade, Greif (1993, 1994) describes the arrangements of Maghrebian and Genoese merchants. As a coalition, they solved the fundamental problem of trade across the Mediterranean area by encouraging shippers responsible for transporting goods to engage in cooperative behavior, ensuring loyalty from shippers through a system of remuneration for cooperation and punishment for deviations from cooperative behavior. The private sector arrangements observed in Côte d'Ivoire, Morocco, and Niger resolve each of the difficulties identified in the previous section. Policy makers must fully understand such arrangements before considering any public policy intervention that could destabilize them. Intermediaries in the food distribution chain have developed informal credit markets for each other. Intermediaries also aggregate prices for nonintegrated markets and form trustworthy relationships that allow product quality to be revealed in the absence of objective quality standards.

Wholesalers and Retailers—Developing Informal Credit Solutions

Combining Repeated Interactions with Punishment Mechanisms in Côte d'Ivoire
In Abidjan, retailers' access to informal credit underpins development of the food distribution system. In particular, a wholesale distribution subsidiary of the Hyajzi Group,[5] the Société nouvelle d'exploitation de marque (SNEM, or New Brand Operating Company), provides access to credit through vendor financing. The Hyajzi Group's market power and its mechanisms to guarantee borrowers' loan repayments share commonalities with the coalition put in place by the Maghrebian merchants. A case study by Lançon and Boyer (2019) describes the Hyajzi Group as follows: "SNEM (Société Nouvelle d'Exploitation de Marque) of the Ivorian family holding company, Hyjazi, distributes as much to supermarkets as to small neighborhood shops, microretailers, and restaurateurs" (p. 38). This description suggests that the group wields substantial market power. The authors also fully describe the punishment and compensation mechanisms SNEM uses for trading and borrowing partners:

> *Romain Hyjazi summarizes SNEM's activities as follows: "We sell to anyone who is solvent!" He explains that SNEM: "works a lot with credit. We work with a lot of salespeople. Clearly, when you work for the first time with a new [customer, service provider, etc.] you give them a few products—we have a small counter that sells cartons of olives—let's say 50 cartons that they pay cash for. If he is reliable, you help him with his stock, you entrust him with*

more and more products on credit. After he grows, it's a little thanks to you, but what is most important is that trust has been established. However, if a buyer of our products becomes insolvent, our relationship will end after ten days [of nonpayment]. Anyway, we cannot operate otherwise; there are very few bank accounts here, so we only work with cash.

(Lançon and Boyer 2019, 40)

Thus the elements that resolved the problem of trade in the Mediterranean region in the 11th century are found in SNEM's implicit credit rules. Repeat relationships reduce a party's incentive to renounce the terms of the deal. Dissuasive punishment mechanisms in the event of deviation—in the case cited, repayment difficulties—enforce the deal. Whereas a medieval Maghrebian family excluded dishonest agents and affected their future earnings by preventing them from being hired again, the Hyjazi family offers customers access to credit, which, without its intermediation, would be more difficult and expensive to get. If not repaid, customers lose the chance to carry on with their business. In view of the Hyjazi Group's market power, not paying back a loan means losing a significant amount of income, thereby distinguishing this credit mechanism from the punishment mechanisms deployed by traditional banks because they only provide credit and do not supply their customers with goods to sell.

Using Social Proximity to Generate Confidence in Niger

The Niamey case study conducted by D'Angelo and Brisson (2019) for this study describes an informal distribution of credit throughout a food distribution chain in Niger:

Without any written documents or contracts, importers massively grant loans to semi-wholesalers on the basis of trust and recover their financing after the goods have been sold. Likewise, retailers reimburse semi-wholesalers only after the goods have been sold. Trust can be established between distant people, crossing borders: thus, Niamey's large merchants can import products from Burkina Faso without having to pay any money or even present a credit guarantee.

(D'Angelo and Brisson 2019, 87)

Experience and reputation[6] create relationships based on trust, and repeated interactions encourage agents to cooperate. Social proximity also seems to be a fundamental element in trustworthy relationships. The Niamey case study explains:

The bond of trust … often rests on a large family, kinship, or ethnicity. Actors' geographic origin and family ties play an important role in creating [trade networks]. Beyond family ties, a common ethnicity makes it possible to establish a bond of trust between two individuals, acting as a guarantee for each party.

(D'Angelo and Brisson 2019, 87–88)

Other research has shown that social proximity encourages cooperative relationships between individuals. Coleman (1990) initially suggested that family ties inspire trusting relationships. Glaeser et al. (2000) show that students at an American university engage in more cooperative behavior with peers of the same nationality or ethnicity than with other peers. Barr (1999) obtains similar results in Zimbabwe. He studied the behavior of villagers who were brought together in the same village in Zimbabwe on land that belonged to large farmers during the Rhodesian government's reign. His work shows that these villagers trust one another less than do individuals who live in villages that have not been recently reorganized. The recent reorganization of the villages and cohabitation by relatively foreign people results in reduced familiarity within the village and therefore greater uncertainty and a loss of trust. To model these elements, Tabellini (2008) proposes a psychological cost to noncooperation that decreases with social distance, creating diversity in cooperative behavior. Individuals engage in cooperative behavior only toward those with whom they are close and not with those from whom they are more distant.

Selling and Lending by Wholesalers in Morocco

In Morocco, private sector contractual arrangements overcome producer difficulties in accessing credit. Aderghal, Lemeilleur, and Romagny (2019) describe how wholesaler traders buy produce:

> A trader can buy "standing" produce, a practice widely used for fruits and herbs, such as mint. This transaction consists of the producer making a preharvest sales contract with a wholesale buyer (or collector-driver trader in remote areas) after the intermediary has identified plots on the farm ... The oral sales agreement may cover one crop or an entire year. For example, wholesale traders buy mint by year, all four crops. The trader thus becomes the owner of the mint and pays the remaining production costs, such as fertilizer or pesticide treatments and irrigation; he also covers the cost of labor for harvesting, sorting, preparing, and transporting mint bundles, as well harvest-related risks. The producer follows a preagreed technical approach to growing the crop, and the trader visits the farm twice a week to monitor the plot's condition ... When a producer sells standing crops, he generally sells at a lower price [than if he sold the crop after harvest]. The producer receives a partial preharvest payment and other payments during the year according to other crop harvests; the trader and producer renegotiate each crop sale according to production quality and market prices.
>
> (Aderghal, Lemeilleur, and Romagny 2019, 33)

Similar to using loans, the practice of selling standing crops allows the producer to move capital in time, receiving harvest profits in advance and spreading them over time. The periodic payments also finance growing costs in anticipation of later profits. Apparently, the standing sales contract reduces moral hazard by creating incentives for the producer to continue making an effort to ensure the quality of his production. Because the trader does not profit from his investment until after the harvest, there is no incentive to engage in uncooperative behavior. The contract's flexibility appears to translate into risk sharing between the producer and the trader, who find a middle ground between a credit financing system in which the producer or the bank bears all risk and a system in which the trader pays the producer and bears all the risk.

Intermediaries—Facilitating the Acquisition of Price Information

The Role of Mobile Phones

Jensen (2007) highlights the nonintegration of markets in many poor countries. As noted earlier, market nonintegration stems from traders' inability to arbitrage differences in price and quality, often because of poor communications infrastructure. According to Jensen (2007):

> Producers and traders often have only limited information, perhaps knowing only the price in a handful of nearby villages or the nearest town, so the potential for inefficiency in the allocation of goods across markets is great. By improving access to information, ICT [information communications and technology] may help poorly functioning markets work better and thereby increase incomes and/or lower consumer prices.
>
> (Jensen 2007, 2)

Jensen's study describes commercial gains made by fishermen in Kerala (India) with the arrival of mobile phones. While still at sea, fishermen use mobile phones to learn about the level of demand in ports where they can dock for the fish they have just caught. Before the arrival of mobile phones, fishermen sometimes chose a port with little demand. They then found it exceedingly difficult to reallocate their catch to places with high demand because of the high transport costs between ports, and so they lost income because of unsold goods.

Mobile phone technology enables better matching of supply and demand, while limiting market research costs (see Aker and Mbiti 2010). In Niger, markets are so poorly integrated (D'Angelo and Brisson 2019) that introducing mobile phones could reduce the cost of acquiring information about markets and improve markets, as in Nigeria and Kenya (Choi, Dutz, and Usman 2019). Thus Aker (2010) notes:

> The introduction of mobile telephony reduces grain price dispersion on the markets by 10 percent. The effect is more marked for market pairs that have higher transport costs because of greater distance and/or poor-quality shipping routes. The effect grows more pronounced over time, which suggests network effects come into play.
>
> (Aker 2010, 47)

The mobile phone effect appears quite widespread in Africa. For example, rural producers in Ghana receive texts showing product sales prices in the capital (Aker and Mbit 2010). Mobile phones allow producers in Uganda to enter new markets, especially for perishable products (Muto and Yamano 2009).[7] Aker (2010) highlights the complementarity between these information technologies and the work of trading intermediaries, finding that the traders' market share is increasing considerably thanks to mobile phones: "Grain traders operating through the mobile phone markets look at a larger number of markets, sell on more markets, and have more commercial contacts than their non-mobile-phone-using peers." The penetration rate of mobile phones is remarkably high in Côte d'Ivoire, Morocco, and Niger. In 2014, 68.2 percent of Nigerien households owned a mobile phone, and in 2017, 99.8 percent of Moroccan households owned one, according to the International Telecommunication Union (ITU 2019), a specialized agency of the United Nations. Although the ITU does not publish mobile phone penetration information for Côte d'Ivoire, Aker and Mbiti (2010) estimate that more than 50 percent of its population subscribed to a mobile phone service in 2008, probably the lower bound for current usage. Despite the widespread diffusion of ICT, private sector arrangements that have organized food supply traders into networks still facilitate the acquisition of price information. For example, even though nearly 100 percent of Moroccan households own a mobile phone, the traders' role is particularly marked in Salé:

Intermediaries play the role of wholesalers. They receive orders from different retailers and work with local production area traders to discover prices. After comparing prices, the intermediary goes to the farm that offers the cheapest prices and ensures delivery to the retailer's store.

(Aderghal, Lemeilleur, and Romagny 2019, 34)

Although the arrival of mobile phones has often reduced the cost of acquiring information about market prices and products, intermediaries in the Salé case match demand to supply in a situation in which information about supply is lacking. They play a role similar to that of mobile phones, reducing transport costs between farms and the time required to collect information.

The Role of Trusted Brokers
The choice of intermediary for long-distance relationships is particularly important because distance amplifies the transaction difficulties, making it harder to inspect product quality and learn market prices. Distance also increases opportunities to engage in uncooperative behavior because it reduces social costs as the links between buyer and seller are more likely weaker. Meanwhile, distance reduces the economic cost of uncooperative behavior because gathering evidence of contract noncompliance is more complicated, particularly in an environment in which contract enforcement mechanisms are underdeveloped.

As noted earlier, the greater the distance between agents, the lower is the probability of a transaction being carried out. ICT could facilitate remote quality inspections and, as already described, help to acquire price information (Choi, Dutz, and Usman 2019). However, even if ICT can help perform some distant quality controls, technology cannot prevent all types of fraud, thereby leaving private sector arrangements with an important role to play. Thus some wholesale traders decide to go see the product themselves, which requires limited distances between sales and production areas:

> The wholesale supply system for mint is shorter. The farms' geographic proximity (30–60 km for Bouknadel-Gharb [wholesale market] and 120 km for Tamaris, near Casablanca) allows wholesalers to carry out transactions directly with producers, without intermediaries, even as one-third of wholesalers from Salé are also producers.
>
> (Aderghal, Lemeilleur, and Romagny 2019, 33)

In other Moroccan markets, trusted brokers reduce the "relationship distance" (Lemeilleur et al. 2019). Most of these intermediaries are "friends," "family," or "associates." They are "present on site to carry out and verify that transactions are properly carried out, … negotiate prices on behalf of the wholesaler, verify the quality and quantities proposed by the producer, load trucks, and pay producers. [For remuneration,] … [t]hey either receive 50 percent of the profits, or receive a variable or fixed commission" (Lemeilleur et al. 2019). Choosing people with close social bonds, such as family or friends, increases the psychological and even the social costs associated with engaging in uncooperative behavior. When traders choose associates or establish specific profit-sharing schemes for agents, the economic cost of uncooperative behavior rises. In both cases, cooperative behavior increases expected gains, resulting in a cooperative equilibrium.

Such an arrangement, which consists of surrounding oneself with trusted intermediaries and sharing social bonds, is also found in Niger's transactions with Nigeria. International transactions make it even harder to enforce contracts because international legal agreements rather than national rules determine enforcement mechanisms, undoubtedly making them more difficult to use. Perhaps for that reason, Hausa traders prefer to trade with members of their ethnic group, especially for international transactions. According to the case study by D'Angelo and Brisson (2019):

> The Hausa network is an example of this phenomenon: trade on the so-called "K²M" highway that connects Maradi (Niger) to Katsina and Kano (Nigeria) is largely facilitated by people on both sides of the border who belong to the same ethnic and religious group and share the same culture and language. This allows trust to be established between Nigerien and Nigerian traders. Trade

works by relay: a trader from one country conveys goods to the border and transfers them to a counterpart from the other country who conveys it towards a market to sell.

(D'Angelo and Brisson 2019, 88)

In an environment in which the cost of resolving disputes is high, using trusted intermediaries ensures the cooperative behavior of business partners at a lower cost. Trusted intermediaries play a central role in distant transactions that are particularly difficult to ensure in the absence of a well-established contract enforcement mechanism. Such intermediaries also reduce the distance-exacerbated cost of acquiring price and quality information.

———

The presence of trusted intermediaries also appears to partially solve the problem of market nonintegration. Thus, despite the great potential of ICT to reduce trade barriers, physical intermediaries continue to play an important role in long-distance transactions. This reinforces the critical role of food system transport costs, as noted in chapter 2. When contract enforcement mechanisms are underdeveloped, the social bonds uniting intermediaries with wholesale sellers and the possibility they can physically meet are decisive for completing transactions (Startz 2018). The fairly low level of interpersonal trust in Côte d'Ivoire, Morocco, and Niger may also explain why traders select intermediaries who belong to a common network. Low trust levels generally prompt large gaps between the high level of trust members of a network give to other members of the same network and their low level of trust for every-one else. These gaps create different equilibriums: a cooperative equilibrium occurs between members of the same network, but not with members of a different network. However, the cost of ensuring contracts and acquiring information—a cost borne by intermediaries—gives rise to a suboptimal cooperative equilibrium. Without these costs, a cooperative equilibrium between the two main trade parties would give them a higher level of well-being.

Substituting Trust between Consumer and Retailer for Certification of Product Quality

When Trust Fills In for Lack of Certification

As just described, repeated interactions encourage cooperative behavior (see Auriol, Balineau, and Bonneton, forthcoming). In Morocco, repeated inter-actions inspire consumer trust in "the quality of products displayed" (Aderghal, Lemeilleur, and Romagny 2019, 24), lending credibility to retailers' assertions about the quality of their goods. These assertions replace deficient or absent food safety and quality certification systems. In effect, quality standards are relatively undeveloped in Morocco, a situation supported by a case study by Aderghal, Lemeilleur, and Romagny (2019):

The concept of product quality certification is not part of Moroccan culture. Rather, it is a new concept recently introduced to the nation. During our fieldwork, we found that almost half of our consumer sample (45 percent of respondents) was unfamiliar with the concept and had never heard of a certified product. Of the other half of respondents who knew about certified products, only 17 percent had bought and consumed such a product. These consumers are often educated people who demand good food hygiene.

(Aderghal, Lemeilleur, and Romagny 2019, 48–49)

Repeated interactions that create trust are quite widespread in Morocco, compensating for the lack of quality standards and certification. The case study by Aderghal, Lemeilleur, and Romagny (2019) found that 32 percent of consumers were relying on trust and their personal relationship with their regular seller as the convention domestically, thereby reducing their uncertainty about the safety and quality of the products they buy. According to Aderghal, Lemeilleur, and Romagny (2019, 44), "This type of agreement is used by people from different socioeconomic categories, including working class, middle class or the affluent—consumers who usually buy from traditional markets." Thus despite the failures of the food quality information system and a fairly low level of interpersonal trust, repeated interactions between consumers and retailers establish trust about product quality.

Family: A Trusted Network that Facilitates Supply and Trade
Short social distance creates trust and facilitates acquiring information about product quality. Members of the same family enjoy the shortest social distance. Studies from several disciplines have examined why family bonds favor interactions. Some scholars use biology-based arguments; others use a sociological approach. Dugatkin (1999, 17–27, cited in Dixit 2004) offers a deterministic and biological vision of cooperative behavior in which family belonging determines certain cooperative behaviors. Anthropologists have also studied trust between family members. Ensminger (1992, cited in Dixit 2004, 61) examines the links between herd owners and their shepherds, showing that owners try to keep a trusted relative in the shepherd camp. Aderghal, Lemeilleur, and Romagny (2019) find that family relationships in Morocco can be a source of food traded between family members living in the country and the city. Beyond an explanation based on solidarity in difficult times, such as between harvests, the authors find that family relationships ensure the quality of products traded:

[For] 50 percent of consumers surveyed, intrafamily trades are very frequent and one way they supply themselves with food products. Several types of products are traded: dairy products, including milk and fermented milk and butter, "beldi" (farm) chicken, grains, including wheat and barley, and fruits and vegetables such as plums, peaches, beans, and peas. The nature of the products traded

depends mainly on the person's area of origin and therefore the most cultivated products in this area ... Product quality is ensured by the trust that exists between family members.

(Aderghal, Lemeilleur, and Romagny 2019, 48)

Effects of the Arrival of Supermarkets on Quality Standards?

Large-scale supermarket brands create trust in their products' quality through practices like those used in high-income countries. Côte d'Ivoire, Morocco, and Niger are seeing the arrival of supermarkets and convenience stores in tandem with the emergence of middle-class consumers who demand quality in the food they buy.[8] However, the market share of these distributors remains small, albeit with wide variations between the countries. For example, in Côte d'Ivoire:

convenience stores, self-service stores, and small and large supermarkets currently account for only 15–20 percent of sales volumes ... Mass consumer distribution is dominated by two large groups, Prosuma and Carré d'Or, plus the Hyjazi Group, which is a supplier, and a new retail competitor operating under the Carrefour brand.

(Lançon and Boyer 2019, 36–37)

In Niger, the appearance of supermarkets is described as "recent" by D'Angelo and Brisson (2019). In Morocco, consumers perceive supermarkets to be guarantors of product quality (Aderghal, Lemeilleur, and Romagny 2019). Only 3 percent of the population thinks that grocery stores and supermarkets "represent high risks for health and hygiene quality," compared with 93 percent who think that microretailers do. The quality of the goods sold by supermarkets is ensured by a specific procurement practice. Thus, although supermarkets procure products from the same sources as traditional distributors, the latter are "characterized by a multitude of intermediaries that mainly manage products sold in bulk, while large distributors vertically integrate products" for most of the products sold, allowing internal quality inspections (Aderghal, Lemeilleur, and Romagny 2019, 51). Thus "modern [tomato] distributors have their own producers who supply tomatoes throughout the year. Their own salaried agents locate in the production areas and act as an interface, ensuring that contracts are honored in terms of price, volume, quality, deadlines, pre-payment, etc." (Aderghal, Lemeilleur, and Romagny 2019, 35). Mint and chicken producers directly supply large-scale Moroccan food distributors. The latter have even obtained waivers that exempt them from having to purchase supplies from wholesale markets. The large distributors' solution to guarantee the quality of the goods sold is not widespread in all countries. Supermarkets in Niger have a different supply structure that goes through wholesalers. In the three countries studied, however, a large distributor's name acts as a trusted brand and seems to take the place of otherwise nonexistent certifications.

———

The marketing practices of supermarkets send a signal about product quality.[9] Ultimately, however, three solutions ensure a quality supply: (1) repeating interactions in order to establish a relationship of trust with a seller; (2) buying from producers in one's own family; and (3) buying from large distributors whose sourcing practices guarantee the quality of the products sold. These solutions compensate for the low level of development of public food quality standards.

The Limits of Private Sector Solutions and Public Institutions' Interventions

The Limits of These Private Sector Solutions

Reputation-Based Solutions That Create Monopoly Situations

The previous section described how weak market integration gives intermediaries a central role in trade because prices are little known from one locality to another and quality standards are poorly developed. These factors complicate long-distance transactions, especially because transport costs are high, as noted in chapter 2. Intermediaries bear the costs of acquiring price and quality information—costs that carry through to the retail price. The resulting higher prices can prevent lower-income consumers from accessing food. Such consumer price increases are exacerbated if intermediaries find themselves in a monopoly position, which happens frequently in situations in which trust and reputation count. It takes time to establish a trustworthy relationship through repeated interactions. Starting a business relationship with a new entrant represents a cost that some traders are unwilling to pay, creating barriers to entry for intermediaries.

Auriol, Balineau, and Bonneton (forthcoming) find that markets in which reputations are important tend to be monopolistic. In Niger, for example, "some large traders monopolize entire product sectors, such as dairy. Thus, major brands such as Nido, Nestlé, Lacstar, and Bridel each have their own wholesaler. Trusted relationships are established over the long term" (D'Angelo and Brisson 2019). This is also the case in Morocco, where Aderghal, Lemeilleur, and Romagny (2019, 9) point out "the rent and oligopoly situations of agents and wholesalers." Their market power blocks the ability of markets to develop. Because wholesale markets have changed little over the past 20 years, "products are mostly sold in bulk, neither packaged nor calibrated" (p. 9).[10]

Competition distortions are also found in supermarkets, where they arise from similar mechanisms of trust between political and economic actors. D'Angelo and Brisson (2019) found that "the owners of these chain stores [two convenience store chains in Niamey, New Market, and Marina Market] are very politically connected and capable of destroying competition by drastically reducing prices. They thus constitute a de facto oligopoly" (p. 63). Economic actors close to political power can probably convey on their companies a profitable economic advantage, as seen in other contexts—see, for example, Fisman (2001). However, more information is needed to describe precisely the forces working for large distributors in Niger. Monopoly or oligopoly situations that harm consumers impose a primary limit on the ability of private sector arrangements to create trust from repeated interactions. However, if government interventions to combat potential monopolies do not have credible alternatives to private sector trust mechanisms, such interventions will be doomed to fail.

Problems Arising from Trading Only with Family or Same Ethnic Group Members
The social proximity requirement of intermediaries reduces the number of possible market matches and undoubtedly curbs the development of some businesses. It also hinders job creation and employment by preventing the hiring of individuals who do not belong to a given family, social, or economic group. According to some empirical studies, ethnicity often leads to hiring discrimination in West Africa—see, for example, Barr and Oduro (2002) on Ghana. Cox and Fafchamps (2007) even suggest that "family and kinship ties can be used ... to consolidate efforts that aim to exclude outsiders from employment." Trade and jobs unrealized for this reason could justify government intervention to the extent that consequent economic value and surplus were not created. The inequalities of opportunity created by these private sector arrangements could also justify public intervention.

Binzel and Fehr (2013) find, moreover, that creating trustworthy relationships through social proximity does not result in optimal levels of cooperation because doing so does not allow cooperative behavior that would have achieved higher levels of well-being for each trading party. The authors conducted an experiment in a Cairo slum, where they played a behavioral economics game. It showed that residents found it as difficult to predict the loyalty of friends (that is, members of their social group) as the loyalty of complete strangers. In fact, the residents tended to underestimate their friends' probability of engaging in cooperative behaviors. Such prediction errors led to a suboptimal cooperative equilibrium. Consequently, it can be assumed that in the food distribution sector, some agents will probably underinvest in their trading activities.

The Higher Interest Rates That Often Result from Using Informal Credit
In the literature, empirical studies have estimated fairly high informal credit rates. Wai (1957) conducted one of the first studies on the subject, documenting informal sector interest rates significantly higher than those adopted by the formal financial system. Ghatak (1975) suggests that market risk justifies these higher rates, which represent a risk premium. In rural South Africa, Dallimore

(2013) recently found high average monthly informal interest rates of about 44 percent. The average hides a very wide disparity in interest rates that ranges from 0 to 600 percent. Similarly, Ngalawa (2014) documents informal interest rates in Malawi that are more than three times higher than formal sector rates. These sometime usurious informal credit market interest rates raise questions about protections for loan applicants. There is a tension between a desire to serve a risky loan market and a concern about offering interest rates that comply with prudential rules. As noted earlier, a creditor's market power, market risk, very often determines interest rates.

Domestic Conventions That Limit the Development of Supermarkets and Processed Food Products

The development of supermarkets and quality standards rests, as noted, on the industrial convention. Some products come up against domestic conventions when challenging private sector arrangements based on repeated interactions that consumers do not wish to change. For example, under the industrial convention consumers' purchase of mint is still underdeveloped in Morocco. According to Aderghal, Lemeilleur, and Romagny (2019):

> Only a few consumers (4 percent of the sample) who are well educated and aware of mint's health safety problems refer to the industrial standards–based industrial convention and buy mint from modern distributors.
>
> (Aderghal, Lemeilleur, and Romagny 2019, 46)

Similarly, consumers do not recognize supermarkets' quality certifications for chicken, which prevents the development of this distribution chain:

> In the case of chicken, the modern tools used to reduce uncertainty [about quality] will be very different from those of traditional markets, because, unlike mint and tomatoes, chicken is not sold in the same condition in both markets: it is often sold alive in the traditional market, while it is slaughtered and packaged in the modern market … [Sixty-three] percent of consumers require seeing a live chicken before choosing to buy it, something possible only in a traditional market where the chicken's price is based on its live weight before slaughter.
>
> (Aderghal, Lemeilleur, and Romagny 2019, 46)

Thus consumers' nonrecognition of the quality standards offered by modern distributors prevents the vertical differentiation of some products sold in supermarkets. It even prevents the expansion of a chicken processing industry that would generate more added value. Thus the predominance of the domestic convention hinders chicken distribution through supermarkets. Here again, as noted earlier, a too-rapid public intervention aimed at modernizing quality standards would run up against Moroccan consumer practices.

Urbanization, Population Growth, and Processed Food Consumption That Reduce the Chances of Buying Food from the Same Retailer

The main forces presented in chapter 1—the rising demand for processed products, urbanization, and population growth—require a reorganization of the last stage of retail food distribution. In the domestic convention relationship in which the consumer trusts a retailer through repeated interactions, increased consumption of processed food makes it harder for that retailer to monitor food quality. In recent decades, the length of value chains has increased considerably because of globalization and fragmentation. Along chains, consumer goods must pass through many hands and borders before reaching a consumer's shopping basket—see, for example, De Backer and Minoudot (2014). This process has made it harder for some retailers to accurately assess the quality of some products they are selling and in turn to guarantee product quality.

Similarly, in the absence of urban farming, urbanization, by fragmenting food product processing and distribution, also affects the marketing of some products and complicates quality monitoring, especially in the absence of standards. For these reasons, urbanization also makes it harder for the retailers to guarantee product quality.

———

Finally, the population boom observed in Côte d'Ivoire, Morocco, and Niger tends to intensify trade frequency, calling for more or larger distributors. The addition of more distributors implies that repeated trust-building interactions with the same intermediary or retailer are harder to achieve. Government interventions have been developed to overcome the many limits of private sector arrangements. The next section presents the solutions, such as support for microfinance, attempts to regulate quality, and systems aimed at disseminating price information in markets.

Interventions by Public Institutions: A Way to Circumvent Difficulties

Support for Microfinance

Microfinance is one of the solutions suggested by Aderghal, Lemeilleur, and Romagny (2019) for overcoming credit constraints in Morocco. The authors believe it important "to imagine a microfinance system for very small retailers in order to allow them to maintain their distribution activity over time and space" (p. 54). Jameel Poverty Action Lab researchers have studied the effectiveness of microfinance in Morocco, finding that clients of the financial services firm al Amana have seen significant increases in their business profits and capital. Their high rates of return (Crépon et al. 2015) are comparable to those observed in other low-income countries by De Mel, McKenzie, and Woodruff (2008) and Banerjee et al. (2015). This finding suggests that credit constraints weigh on the Moroccan economy by preventing what would be profitable microlenders from entering the market.

However, these gains in business profitability do not translate directly into consumption gains. A meta-analysis of microfinance systems by Banerjee, Karlan, and Zinman (2015) finds that consumption gains are low in Côte d'Ivoire, Morocco, and Niger. The authors argue that this outcome results from entrepreneurial work replacing paid work. Although microfinance appears to foster more competition along the food distribution chain, its introduction will not necessarily translate into economic gains for borrowers. Furthermore, microfinance uptake is often quite low. For example, Crépon et al. (2015) find that in the areas where al Amana launched microlending, uptake was less than 20 percent. Low use may be explained by highly diverse returns from entrepreneurial activities, including no profit or even losses. Entrepreneurs are probably aware of the riskiness of their efforts. For the risk-averse, the high volatility of returns can prevent them from borrowing even when financing is available. Therefore, microfinance alone is probably insufficient to solve credit constraints. Notably, recent research tends to show that using psychometric tests to select entrepreneur borrowers tends to reduce the default rate of loans issued by credit institutions—see, for example, Arraiz et al. (2017). Thus improving the selection of borrowers could reduce lenders' risk premiums. In turn, providing assistance in selecting borrowers with the highest probability of success would likely increase lending efficiency.

The Nigerien government is tackling other difficulties encountered by start-ups. According to D'Angelo and Brisson (2019), it has "put many provisions in place to facilitate commercial activities, reducing the constituent parts necessary for the creation of a limited liability corporation (LLC) and setting up a dedicated service counter" (p. 51). The complexity of administrative procedures in low-income countries has often been blamed for curbing the creation of formal businesses (Benhassine et al. 2017; De Soto 2000; Djankov et al. 2002).

Attempts to Regulate Quality

Morocco's Example
Aderghal, Lemeilleur, and Romagny (2019) have analyzed quality regulation in Morocco, focusing on mint distribution, which garnered bad news coverage about dirty irrigation water, excessive pesticide use, and even use of prohibited products, among other concerns. Officials first responded to these highly publicized health crises by creating an inspection and certification body in 2009, the Office national de sécurité sanitaire des produits alimentaires (ONSSA, or National Office for the Sanitary Safety of Food Products). The Ministry of Agriculture oversees ONSSA, a financially autonomous institution that inspects

food and monitors food safety by performing analyses, checking food handler hygiene, approving pesticides and fertilizers, certifying seeds, inspecting animal products, and issuing food safety and hygiene certifications to establishments that produce, import, or export food products (Aderghal, Lemeilleur, and Romagny 2019, 39). In addition to creating ONSSA, in March 2010 Morocco promulgated a law that frames the quality of food offered for sale. The law sets out "the conditions under which primary products, food products, and animal feed must be handled, treated, processed, packaged, conditioned, transported, stored, distributed, displayed for sale, or exported in order to qualify as a safe product." The law further establishes "general rules of hygiene, sanitation, use of cleaning products and disinfection, [and] admissible contamination thresholds," and sets out "mandatory rules for informing the consumer, in particular through [quality certification] labeling." It also makes supply chain traceability compulsory and empowers food distributors by forcing companies to set up self-inspection and quality management systems that previously operated under the government's purview.

The 2010 law and ONSSA complement one another, empowering firms by giving them defined obligations and sanctions and by providing the means to exercise these responsibilities. ONSSA grants food safety and hygiene certifications to establishments responsible for tracing and labeling food products. More recent decrees have included regulations and quality standards for specific issues. Examples are the organic farming standards issued in January 2013 and the January 2014 decree setting the maximum authorized pesticide residue limits. In addition, inspections of exported products are carried out in the importing country. ONSSA provides support to "go tracing back to the exporter and producer" and applies sanctions first by issuing a warning and then by banning exports. ONSSA expanded its export inspection capacity through collaboration with European Union import services (Europe is Morocco's main export destination). However, inspections of products intended for the domestic market are much less effective: "Samples are rarely analyzed, except for the most-consumed products and some samples from souks, but never from grocery stores, and no sanction is applied, because the product is not traceable to the producer" (Aderghal, Lemeilleur, and Romagny 2019, 43).

To increase retail product quality, one solution may be to require larger supermarkets and wholesalers to source inspected and traceable products. At the same time, ONSSA is attempting to reinforce the credibility of its producer sanctions, which is particularly difficult because products lack traceability. Meanwhile, the institution is developing producer awareness campaigns. Its "phytosanitary tours" consist of giving producers a list of approved pesticides, dosing information, and preharvest pesticide application deadlines. Each year, ONSSA conducts about 2,000 tours nationally and also organizes additional training and awareness days. This program began in 2005, but from 2010 to

2014 it was taken over by the Food and Agriculture Organization, creating the Farmer Field School. ONSSA also advises producers about suppliers of approved inputs.

Measures Taken by the Nigerien Government
In Niger, establishing quality standards begins by raising producer awareness. The Nigerien Ministry of Finance and Ministry of Agriculture oversee a state-operated enterprise, the Réseau national des chambres d'agriculture du Niger (RECA, or National Network of Chambers of Agriculture), which was set up in 2009. Supported by the Nigerien government and international donors, RECA conducts training and awareness-raising actions in order to reduce pesticide use, among other concerns (D'Angelo and Brisson 2019). In addition, a "Nigeriens Nourish Nigeriens" initiative promotes food quality inspections to improve the quality of the nation's products and to impose standards on imports and exports. This presidential-level initiative gains strength from the involvement of several ministries. The government also may support a hygiene inspection system for marketplaces (D'Angelo and Brisson 2019). However, Niger currently conducts few inspections. Although responsibility for doing so rests with the Office des Produits Vivriers du Niger (OPVN, or Nigerien Food Products Office), which is overseen by the Ministry of Commerce, OPVN has not yet implemented any inspections or standards for international or domestic trade. OPVN, which ensures a food supply for needy populations, only inspects product quality and compliance with criteria specified in contracts when redistributing products during food crises. It currently has three inspection laboratories: a central one in Niamey, one in Zinder for the Maradi and Diffa regions, and one in Tahoua that also covers the Agadez region. It is seeking to create one laboratory for each region for a total of eight.

Niger also has an effective onion and cowpea traceability tool, and expansion of the system to other products is under discussion. According to D'Angelo and Brisson (2019), "This system, which has been in place for about three years, allows some traceability of products from farm to retailer; it also allows the government to levy and collect taxes through centralized collection facilities. Located near farms, these facilities aggregate production from all producers in the area for transport and sale through various channels. While each channel has its own driver, all drivers follow the same circuit since there are few roads in the area. All production-related taxes are paid at these collection facilities" (p. 99). The facilities also serve as product tracing points. Even if no documentation supports the idea, a dense network of centralized collection facilities would help by hosting product traceability and quality certification systems. Thus setting up inspection agents or laboratories in these facilities could make it possible for producers to receive product quality certifications when they receive tax payment receipts—a first step toward guaranteeing product quality for the consumer.

Other Solutions from Similar Contexts
In other countries, other types of public interventions to increase product quality information include quality certifications and short distribution chains (see Auriol, Balineau, and Bonneton, forthcoming, for a complete view of quality problems in developing countries). Certifications allow consumers to quickly identify quality levels by grouping a set of products that meet the same production, safety, and hygiene requirements from farm to retail store. However, consumers must be taught to recognize these quality signals. Short distribution chains also increase information about products, ensuring traceability from farm to the point of consumption. Short chain distributors have fewer steps between producers and consumers, making it easier for retailers to guarantee the quality of the products they sell.

Market Information Systems to Collect Price Information for Dissemination
One of the first steps needed when integrating markets is to make price information accessible. With this in mind, market information systems have emerged in many Sub-Saharan African countries. The Nigerien Ministry of Commerce has set up an MIS with wholesalers to record the stocks and prices of basic necessities such as grains, coffee, tea, milk, and sugar. Inspection agents make biweekly readings to collect data and transmit it to the National Institute of Statistics, which produces a price table. Everyone concerned—public officials, wholesalers, retailers, and consumers—can receive this information. David-Benz et al. (2012) have identified two market information systems in Côte d'Ivoire (MIS2G 2015). The Office d'aide à la commercialisation des produits vivriers (OCPV, or Food Products Marketing Office) set up the first MIS in 1986 "with the aim of supplying all food sector operators—producers, traders, government officials, and institutions—with reliable market, economic, and statistical data" (WFP and OCPV 2007). The Association nationale des organisations professionnelles agricoles de Côte d'Ivoire (ANOPACI, or National Association of Professional Agricultural Organizations of Côte d'Ivoire) set up the second MIS in 2002. It follows "technical, economic (wholesale prices), and commercial (retail prices, volumes, offers) information for four main sectors: pineapples and bananas, food crops, market gardening, and livestock." Inter-réseaux (2008) describes how the ANOPACI MIS collects and disseminates information (box 3.1). Inspectors collect information on a weekly basis, and the information is broadcast through posters, a quarterly bulletin, and the radio (Inter-réseaux 2007).

The desire to create a centralized information system for prices and quality controls is often put forward as one of the reasons to set up wholesale markets or to require that products be sold through them. However, the need for regulation of wholesale prices and for information declines, especially for domestic markets, with the development of the other institutions described here, including ICT, quality certifications, and domestic or industrial conventions. Consequently, wholesale marketplaces persist more as platforms for product grouping and unloading, or for collecting taxes (see chapter 2).

BOX 3.1

The ANOPACI MIS Information Collection Method

The ANOPACI market information system (MIS) operates through village information points, or VIPs (Inter-réseaux 2008). In 2006 ANOPACI had 15 operational VIPs covering approximately 25 of the 58 departments in Côte d'Ivoire.

Information Collection Method

The VIP agent visits four or five rural markets every week between 7:00 a.m. and 11:00 a.m. to collect information on consumer prices, wholesale prices, and average trends on product availability, supply, and demand. The agent meets three different sellers for each product. He notes prices on a data collection sheet and uses a small scale to convert traditional units to conventional units. For each product, he also comments on the quality, quantity, and evolution of the market compared with the previous week. To make the data more reliable, the VIP agent combines product information from sellers with information from consumers (buyers). The agent also collects wholesale prices and assesses the main local wholesalers' stocks.

Information Processing and Dissemination Method

Once the VIP agent completes the data collection sheets for a market, he processes the data electronically by editing a summary sheet that shows the maximum, minimum, and average prices. He uses the summary to disseminate information via the local rural radio station and transmits it to VIP headquarters where the information can be stored and exchanged between VIPs at the department level. The information is used to create media communications, including short-term bulletins, newsletters, and other means of information dissemination. The information exchanged between VIPs mainly concerns agricultural product prices in each department's markets, as well as selling and buying quantities, prices, and quality. All VIPs are connected to the internet. Currently, 15 rural radio stations broadcast agricultural product prices, availability, and demand as part of the MIS.

Source: Kouao and Sindikubwabo 2007.

Conclusion

Transport costs limit the ability of consumers and suppliers to arbitrage prices, thereby limiting the ability of food markets to function in an optimal way, as seen in chapter 2. The negative effect of transport costs is reinforced when uncertainty about price and quality makes trading in person even more important. To allay uncertainty in some way other than by bearing prohibitive transport costs, multiple private sector arrangements are being put into place, particularly intermediation, trustworthy relationships, reputation, vertical integration, and informal lending. These private sector arrangements can result in excessive market power that negatively affects some players, particularly consumers. However, modernizing public policy actions, such as providing microfinance, market information systems, mobile telephony, official quality standards, and monopoly and antitrust regulation, must be implemented with caution and coordination. Otherwise, they risk calling fragile market institutions and equilibria into question without solid answers or alternatives.

Notes

1. For example, gravity equations.
2. The World Values Survey brings together academics from several world regions, aiming to collect information on changing values and their effects on social and political life in most countries.
3. However, current dynamics favor the development of more efficient financial systems in these countries. Successive waves of the Global Financial Inclusion Database of the World Bank (2017b) show an improvement in each of these metrics.
4. Dixit refers, for example, to a survey conducted by Hendley and Murrell (2003) of Romanian countries in transition. When asked to classify the mechanisms that facilitate their transactions, more than half highlighted bilateral mechanisms that do not involve the state. Similarly, a study by Ellickson (1991) focuses on a group of Northern California farmers who attempt to resolve quarrels over uncontrolled herd movements amicably and bilaterally. If punishment is to take place, it is primarily social and involves the spread of rumors.
5. Lançon and Boyer (2019) describe the group as follows: "An Ivorian family-run holding company, Hyjazi Group was founded in 1981 by brothers Hassan and Samih, who are now euro billionaires … The Hyjazi Group has 4000 employees and is composed of 13 companies … including the New Brand Operating Company (SNEM) … a key player in the Abidjan food distribution sector and the wholesaling subsidiary of the Hyjazi Group" (p. 38).
6. See Auriol, Balineau, and Bonneton (forthcoming) for a formal explanation of how reputations are established.
7. This literature has recently been revisited and is the subject of academic debate. See, for example, Mitra et al. (2018).

8. Note, however, that Lançon and Boyer (2019) conclude that the various distribution channels do not segment consumers according to a standard of living based on the indicator "owns a refrigerator," which could be more informative.
9. However, supermarkets still lack certain essential signals for part of the population. For example, because large companies find it difficult to achieve halal standards of slaughter (Aderghal, Lemeilleur, and Romagny 2019), some Moroccan consumers turn away from supermarkets for their meat supply.
10. The lack of wholesale market development in Morocco is linked to reasons other than the monopolistic tendency of markets where reputation matters. Rousseau, Boyet, and Harroud (2019) study the political tensions between a modernizing and a conservative vision of food governance in Morocco, which crystallize around wholesale market reforms (see chapter 2).

References

Abate, G. T., T. Bernar, A. de Brauw, and N. Minot. 2018. "The Impact of the Use of New Technologies on Farmers' Wheat Yield in Ethiopia: Evidence from a Randomized Control Trial." *Agricultural Economics* 49 (4): 409–21.

Aderghal, M., S. Lemeilleur, and B. Romagny. 2019. "Contribution des systèmes de distribution alimentaire à la sécurité alimentaire des villes: étude de cas sur l'agglomération de Rabat (Maroc)" [The contribution of food distribution systems to urban food security: Case study of Rabat, Morocco]. Notes techniques, No. 48, Agence française de développement, Paris, February. https://www.afd.fr/fr/nt-48-systeme-alimentaire-qualite-sanitaire-aderghal-lemeilleur-romagny.

Aker, J. C. 2010. "Information from Markets Near and Far: Mobile Phones and Agricultural Markets in Niger." *American Economic Journal: Applied Economics* 2 (3): 46–59.

Aker, J. C., and I. M. Mbiti. 2010. "Mobile Phones and Economic Development in Africa." *Journal of Economic Perspectives* 24 (3): 207–32.

Akerlof, G. 1970. "The Market for Lemons: Quality Uncertainty and the Market Mechanism." *Quarterly Journal of Economics* 84 (3): 488–500.

Algan, Y., and P. Cahuc. 2014. "Trust, Well-Being and Growth: New Evidence and Policy Implications." In *Handbook of Economic Growth*, edited by P. Aghion and S. N. Durlauf, 49–120. Amsterdam: Elsevier Science.

Aloui, O., and L. Kenny. 2005. "The Cost of Compliance with SPS Standards for Moroccan Exports: A Case Study." Agricultural and Rural Development Discussion Paper, World Bank, Washington, DC.

Araujo, C., C. Araujo-Bonjean, and S. Brunelin. 2012. "Alert at Maradi: Preventing Food Crises by Using Price Signals." *World Development* 40 (9): 1882–94.

Arraiz, I., M. Bruhn, C. Ruiz Ortega, and R. M. Stucchi. 2017. "Are Psychometric Tools a Viable Screening Method for Small and Medium-Size Enterprise Lending? Evidence from Peru." Policy Research Working Paper 8276, Impact Evaluation Series, World Bank, Washington, DC.

Arrow, K. 1972. "Gifts and Exchanges." *Philosophy and Public Affairs* 1 (4): 343–62.

Atkin, D., B. Faber, and M. Gonzalez-Navarro. 2018. "Retail Globalization and Household Welfare: Evidence from Mexico." *Journal of Political Economy* 126 (1): 1–73.

Auriol, A., G. Balineau, and N. Bonneton. Forthcoming. "The Economics of Quality in Developing Countries in a Global Value Chains World."

Banerjee, A., E. Duflo, C. Kinnan, and R. Glennerster. 2015. "The Miracle of Microfinance? Evidence from a Randomized Evaluation." *American Economic Journal: Applied Economics* 7 (1): 22–53.

Banerjee, A., D. Karlan, and J. Zinman. 2015. "Six Randomized Evaluations of Microcredit: Introduction and Further Steps." *American Economic Journal: Applied Economics* 7 (1): 1–21.

Barr, A. 1999. "Familiarity and Trust: An Experimental Investigation." CSAE Working Paper Series, No. 23, Centre for the Study of African Economies, Oxford University, Oxford, U.K.

Barr, A., and A. Oduro. 2002. "Ethnic Fractionalization in an African Labour Market." *Journal of Development Economics* 68 (2): 355–79.

Benhassine, N., D. McKenzie, V. Pouliquen, and M. Santini. 2017. "Does Inducing Informal Firms to Formalize Make Sense? Experimental Evidence from Benin." *Journal of Public Economics* 57 (C): 1–14.

Berg, J., J. Dickhaut, and K. McCabe. 1995. "Trust, Reciprocity, and Social-History." *Games and Economic Behavior* 10 (1): 122–42.

Binzel, C., and D. Fehr. 2013. "Social Distance and Trust: Experimental Evidence from a Slum in Cairo." *Journal of Development Economics* 103: 99–106.

Boltanski, O., and L. Tévenot. 1991. *De la justifcation: les économies de la grandeur* [*Justification: Economies of scale*]. Paris: Gallimard.

Bowles, S., R. Boyd, H. Gintis, and E. Fehr. 2005. "Moral Sentiments and Material Interests: Origins, Evidence, and Consequences." In *Moral Sentiments and Material Interests*, edited by H. Gintis, S. Bowles, R. Boyd, and E. Fehr, 3–40. Cambridge, MA: MIT Press.

Bowles, S., and H. Gintis. 2007. "Cooperation." In *The New Palgrave Dictionary of Economics*, edited by L. Blume and S. Durlauf. London: Palgrave Macmillan UK.

Brunelin, S., and A. Portugal-Perez. 2013. "Food Markets and Barriers to Regional Integration in West Africa." Unpublished document, Africa Region, World Bank, Washington, DC.

Cahuc, P., and Y. Algan. 2014. "Trust, Institutions, and Economic Development." In *Handbook of Economic Growth*, Vol. 2A, edited by S. Durlauf and P. Aghion. Oxford, U.K., and San Diego, CA: Elsevier.

Calmette, F. Forthcoming. "Le rôle des marchés dans l'approvisionnement alimentaire des villes: un agenda de recherche basé sur la théorie" [The role of markets in urban food supply: A research agenda based on theory]. Papiers de recherche, Agence française de développement, Paris.

Camara, A. 2016. "Dans quelle mesure la distance est déterminante dans les réseaux d'approvisionnement alimentaire de la ville d'aujourd'hui ? Application au cas de la ville d'Abidjan" [How decisive is distance in today's urban food supply networks? A look at the case of Abidjan]. PhD diss., SupAgro and Cirad, Montpellier.

Casaburi, L., and J. Willis. 2018. "Time vs. State in Insurance: Experimental Evidence from Contract Farming in Kenya." *American Economic Review* 108 (12): 3778–813.

Choi, J., M. Dutz, and Z. Usman. 2019. "The Future of Work in Africa: Harnessing the Potential of Digital Technologies for All." World Bank, Washington, DC. https://openknowledge.worldbank.org/handle/10986/32124 License: CC BY 3.0 IGO.

Coleman, J. 1990. *Foundations of Social Theory*. Cambridge, MA: Harvard University Press.

Cox, D., and M. Fafchamps. 2007. "Extended Family and Kinship Networks: Economic Insights and Evolutionary Directions." In *Handbook of Development Economics*, edited by H. Chenery and T. N. Srinivasan, chap. 58. Amsterdam: Elsevier.

Crépon, B., F. Devoto, E. Duflo, and W. Parienté. 2015. "Estimating the Impact of Micro-credit on Those Who Take It Up: Evidence from a Randomized Experiment in Morocco." *American Economic Journal: Applied Economics* 7 (1): 123–50.

D'Angelo, L., and E. Brisson. 2019. "Systèmes d'approvisionnement et de distribution alimentaires: étude de cas sur la ville de Niamey (Niger)" [Food supply and distribution systems: Case study on the city of Niamey, Niger]. Notes techniques, No. 50, Agence française de développement, Paris, February. https://www.afd.fr/fr/nt-50-marche-alimentation-distribution-groupe8-brisson-emile-geay-dangelo.

Dallimore, A. 2013. "Banking on the Poor: Savings, Poverty and Access to Financial Services in Rural South Africa." PhD diss., London School of Economics.

David-Benz, H., J. Egg, F. Galtier, J. Rakotoson, Y. Shen, and A. Kizito. 2012. "Les systèmes d'information sur les marchés agricoles en Afrique subsaharienne" [Agricultural markets information systems in Sub-Saharan Africa]. Focales AFD, Agence française de développement, Paris.

De Backer, K., and S. Miroudot. 2014. "Mapping Global Value Chains." ECB Working Paper, No. 1677, European Central Bank (ECB), Frankfurt. https://ssrn.com/abstract=2436411.

De Mel, S., D. McKenzie, and C. Woodruff. 2008. "Returns to Capital in Microenterprises: Evidence from a Field Experiment." *Quarterly Journal of Economics* 123 (4): 1329–72.

De Soto, H. 2000. *The Mystery of Capital: Why Capitalism Triumphs in the West and Fails Everywhere Else*. London: Basic Books.

Dethier, J.-J., and A. Effenberger. 2011. "Agriculture and Development: A Brief Review of the Literature." *Economic Systems* 36 (2): 175–205.

Dixit, A. K. 2004. *Lawlessness and Economics: Alternative Modes of Governance*. Princeton, NJ: Princeton University Press.

Djankov, S., R. La Porta, F. Lopez-de-Silanes, and A. Shleifer. 2002. "The Regulation of Entry." *Quarterly Journal of Economics* 117 (1): 1–37.

Dugatkin, L. 1999. *Cheating Monkeys and Citizen Bees: The Nature of Cooperation in Animals and Humans*. New York: Simon and Schuster.

Ellickson, R. C. 1991. *Order without Law: How Neighbors Settle Disputes*. Cambridge, MA: Harvard University Press.

Ensminger, J. 1992. *Making a Market: The Institutional Transformation of an African Society*. Cambridge, U.K.: Cambridge University Press.

Fackler, P. L., and B. Goodwin. 2001. "Spatial Price Analysis." In *Handbook of Agricultural Economics*, Vol. 1, No. 2, edited by G. C. Rausser and B. L. Garneder. Paris: Elsevier.

Fehr, E. 2009. "On the Economics and Biology of Trust." Presidential address at 2008 meeting of European Economic Association. *Journal of the European Economic Association* 7 (2–3): 235–66.

Fisman, R. 2001. "Estimating the Value of Political Connections." *American Economic Review* 91 (4): 1095–1102.

Ghatak, S. 1975. "Rural Interest Rates in the Indian Economy." *Journal of Development Studies* 11 (3): 190–201.

Glaeser, E., D. Laibson, J. Scheinkman, and C. Soutter. 2000. "Measuring Trust." *Quarterly Journal of Economics* 115 (3): 811–46.

Greif, A. 1993. "Contract Enforceability and Economic Institutions in Early Trade: The Maghrebi Traders' Coalition." *American Economic Review* 83 (3): 525–48.

Greif, A. 1994. "Cultural Beliefs and the Organization of Society: A Historical and Theoretical Reflection on Collectivist and Individualist Societies." *Journal of Political Economy* 102 (5): 912–50.

Greif, A. 2000. "The Fundamental Problem of Exchange: A Research Agenda in Historical Institutional Analysis." *European Review of Economic History* 4 (3): 251–84.

Gupta, S., and R. Mueller. 1982. "Analyzing the Pricing Efficiency in Spatial Markets: Concept and Application." *European Review of Agricultural Economics* 9 (3): 301–12.

Hendley, K., and P. Murrell. 2003. "Which Mechanisms Support the Fulfillment of Sales Agreement? Asking Decision-makers in Firms." *Economics Letters* 78 (1): 49–54.

Inglehart, R., C. Haerpfer, A. Moreno, C. Welzel, K. Kizilova, J. Diez-Medrano, M. Lagos, et al., eds. 2014. World Values Survey: Round Six—Country-Pooled Datafile Version, JD Systems Institute, Madrid. http://www.worldvaluessurvey.org/WVSDocumentation WV6.jsp.

Inter-réseaux. 2007. "Projet SIM note conjoncturelle trimestrielle" [MIS Project quarterly newletter]. No. 1. http://www.inter-reseaux.org/IMG/pdf/CI_ANOPACI__Note _Trimestrielle.pdf.

Inter-réseaux. 2008. "Les Systèmes d'Information de Marché (SIM): Des dispositifs efficaces pour une meilleure transparence des marchés?" [Market Information Systems (MIS): Effective means to improve market transparency?]. http://www .inter-reseaux.org/IMG/pdf_SIM.pdf.

Jensen, R. 2007. "The Digital Provide: Information (Technology), Market Performance, and Welfare in the South Indian Fisheries Sector." *Quarterly Journal of Economics* 122 (3): 879–924.

Knack, S., and P. Keefer. 1997. "Does Social Capital Have an Economic Payoff? A Cross-Country Investigation." *Quarterly Journal of Economics* 112 (4): 1252–88.

Kouao, S., and I. Sindikubwabo. 2007. "Le système d'information sur les marchés: condition nécessaire à la réussite de nos opérations de commercialisation. L'expérience de l'ANOPACI" [The market information system: A necessary condition for the success of our marketing operations. ANOPACI's experience]. Paper presented at Bamako Regional Forum, January 16–18, Inter-réseaux Développement rural, CTA, AFDI.

Lançon, F., and A. Boyer. 2019. "Contribution des systèmes de distribution alimentaire à la sécurité alimentaire des villes: étude de cas sur l'agglomération d'Abidjan (Côte d'Ivoire)" [The contribution of food distribution systems to urban food security: Case study of Abidjan, Côte d'Ivoire]. Notes techniques, No. 49, February, Agence française de développement, Paris. https://www.afd.fr/fr/nt-49-systeme-alimentaire-urbanisation-abidjan-lancon-boyer.

Lemeilleur, S., M. Aderghal, O. Jenani, A. Binane, M. Berja, Y. Medaoui, and P. Moustier. 2019. "La distance est-elle toujours importante pour organiser l'approvisionnement alimentaire urbain? Le cas de l'agglomération de Rabat" [Is distance always important for urban food supply production? The case of Greater Rabat]. Papiers de recherche, No. 91, Agence française de développement, Paris. https://www.afd.fr/fr/la-distance-est-elle-toujours-importante-pour-organiser-lapprovisionnement-alimentaire-urbain-le-cas-de-lagglomeration-de-rabat.

MIS2G. 2015. "MIS's List." Agricultural Research Centre for International Development (CIRAD), Madascar. http://www.sim2g.org/mis_network.

Mitra, S., D. Mookherjee, M. Torero, and S. Visaria. 2018. "Asymmetric Information and Middleman Margins: An Experiment with Indian Potato Farmers." *Review of Economics and Statistics* 100 (1): 1–13.

Muto, M., and T. Yamano. 2009. "The Impact of Mobile Phone Coverage Expansion on Market Participation: Panel Data Evidence from Uganda." *World Development* 37 (12): 1887–96.

Ngalawa, H. 2014. "A Portrait of Informal Sector Credit and Interest Rates in Malawi." Interpolated Monthly Time Series, Working Paper, No. 446, Economic Research Southern Africa, Cape Town. https://econrsa.org/system/files/publications/working_papers/working_paper_446.pdf.

Rousseau, M., A. Boyet, and T. Harroud. 2019. "Le makhzen et le marché de gros: la politique d'approvisionnement des villes marocaines entre contrôle social et néolibéralisme" [The governing elite and the wholesale market: The supply policy of Moroccan cities straddles social control and neoliberalism]. Papiers de recherche, No. 92, Agence française de développement, Paris. https://www.afd.fr/fr/le-makhzen-et-le-marche-de-gros-la-politique-dapprovisionnement-des-villes-marocaines-entre-controle-social-et-neoliberalisme.

Startz, M. 2018. "The Value of Face-to-Face: Search and Contracting Problems in Nigerian Trade." Working paper, World Trade Organization, Geneva. https://www.wto.org/english/news_e/news17_e/startz_stud_14sep17_e.pdf.

Stigler, G. 1961. "The Economics of Information." *Journal of Political Economy* 69 (3): 213–25.

Sylvander, B. 1997. "Le rôle de la certification dans les changements de régime de coordination: l'agriculture biologique du réseau à l'industrie" [The role of certification in changing a coordination regime: Organic farming from network to industry]. *Revue d'économie industrielle* No. 80, 2d quarter, 47–66.

Tabellini, G. 2008. "Institutions and Culture." *Journal of the European Economic Association, Papers and Proceedings* 6 (2-3): 255–94.

Tefft, J. F., M. Jonasova, R. T. O. A. Adjao, and A. M. Morgan. 2017. *Food Systems for an Urbanizing World: Knowledge Product.* Washington, DC: World Bank and Food and Agriculture Organization of the United Nations. http://documents.worldbank.org /curated/en/454961511210702794/Food-systems-for-an-urbanizing-world-knowledge -product.

Wai, U. T. 1957. "Interest Rates Outside the Organized Money Markets of Underdeveloped Countries." IMF Staff Papers, No. 6, International Monetary Fund (IMF), Washington, DC.

WFP (World Food Programme) and OCPV (Bureau de Côte d'Ivoire Office d'aide à la commercialisation des produits vivriers). 2007. "Note conjointe sur l'évolution des prix de marché" [Joint newsletter on market price trends]. No. 3, WFP, Abidjan. http://www.inter-reseaux.org/IMG/pdf/Bulletin_OCPV-PAM_3.pdf.

World Bank. 2017a. Rule of Law Index. https://databank.worldbank.org/databases /rule-of-law.

World Bank. 2017b. Global Financial Inclusion (Global Findex) Database. https://data catalog.worldbank.org/dataset/global-financial-inclusion-global-findex-database.

World Bank. 2019. Ease of Doing Business Rankings (database). https://www.doing business.org/en/rankings.

World Bank. 2020. *World Development Report 2020: Trading for Development in the Age of Global Value Chains.* Washington, DC: World Bank.